English Learners at the Top of the Class

English Learners at the Top of the Class

Edited by Mayra C. Daniel

ROWMAN & LITTLEFIELD
Lanham • Boulder • New York • London

Published by Rowman & Littlefield
A wholly owned subsidiary of The Rowman & Littlefield Publishing Group, Inc.
4501 Forbes Boulevard, Suite 200, Lanham, Maryland 20706
www.rowman.com

Unit A, Whitacre Mews, 26-34 Stannary Street, London SE11 4AB

Copyright © 2017 by Mayra C. Daniel

All rights reserved. No part of this book may be reproduced in any form or by any electronic or mechanical means, including information storage and retrieval systems, without written permission from the publisher, except by a reviewer who may quote passages in a review.

British Library Cataloguing in Publication Information Available

Library of Congress Cataloging-in-Publication Data

978-1-4758-3683-7 (cloth : alk. paper)
978-1-4758-3684-4 (pbk. : alk. paper)
978-1-4758-3685-1 (electronic)

∞ ™ The paper used in this publication meets the minimum requirements of American National Standard for Information Sciences Permanence of Paper for Printed Library Materials, ANSI/NISO Z39.48-1992.

Printed in the United States of America

Contents

Preface	ix
Acknowledgments	xiii
Foreword	xv
Introduction	xvii

I: Processes in Reading and Selection of Authentic Literature

1. What Teachers of ELs Need to Consider Regarding Nonverbal Processes in Reading Comprehension — 3
   Fabiola P. Ehlers-Zavala
2. Culturally Relevant Literature for Multilingual Classrooms — 15
   Melanie Koss and Mayra C. Daniel

II: Disciplinary Literacies

3. Empowering ELs through Purposeful Writing Instruction in Content Areas — 33
   Guang-Lea Lee
4. Literacy-Focused Science Instruction for Young English Learners — 53
   Carolyn Riley and Rodney Fitzgerald
5. Supporting ELs in Learning to Write Scientifically: A Genre-Based Approach — 67
   Zhihui Fang, Brittany Adams, Cuiying Li, Caitlin Gallingane, Soowon Jo, Maureen Fennessy, and Suzanne Chapman
6. Student-Centered Approaches for Teaching Social Studies to English Learners — 83
   Mayra C. Daniel, Carolyn Riley, and Teresa Kruger

III: Evaluation for Learning

7 Assessing English Learner Readers at Levels K–12   103
   Kathrine Crane Rockwell and Rona F. Flippo

References   119

About the Editor   129

List of Contributors   131

Preface

In *English Learners at the Top of the Class*, chapter authors address the effects of the changing demographics in the United States on the increasingly diverse composition of student populations in schools. They encourage teachers to examine how and why instructional paradigms need to offer culturally relevant ways for students to learn. They challenge teachers to be designers of curriculum and to trust their instincts and knowledge.

All of us who wrote chapters identify the teachers who read this book as our collaborators. You are our co-researchers because you know your students and their communities and can identify how to aid English learners (ELs) to overcome situated challenges. This book continues a conversation begun with teachers and teacher candidates in book one of this series: *Culture, Language, and Curricular Choices: What Teachers Need to Know about Planning Instruction for English Learners*.

We need to remember that ELs' experiences within their communities of origin are different from those of the monolingual students'. For them, interacting in several languages may be the norm in daily life. ELs' intercultural experiences are enhanced by this plurilingualism. Inherent in pluricultural ways of thinking and behaving is the knowledge that the individual is free to enter others' worlds. ELs must be provided spaces to develop an awareness that their lives matter. Difference does not equate to one person having more or fewer rights than another.

Teachers must ensure social justice paradigms meet ELs' educational and affective needs (Ehlers-Zavala, chapter 1). There are differences between background and experiential knowledge, and between schooled knowledge and funds of knowledge. It is necessary to recognize and consider the knowledge that ELs bring to school when planning instruction: what the students studied previously in their formal schooling and the knowledge they learned from the people in their circles of influence (Koss & Daniel, chapter 2).

The discipline-specific methods for instruction provided highlight the need for new ways of thinking about learners' knowledge base and what the population changes demand in instructional practices. Teachers know they have to teach more than isolated vocabulary. They are also aware that context clues will not provide all the aids to comprehension needed by ELs (Riley & Fitzgerald, chapter 4). The context of lessons and assessments must be culturally relevant to the learners so that they are able to comprehend and showcase their academic growth (Crane Rockwell & Flippo, chapter 7).

ELs will learn more and be evaluated fairly when lessons address all language modalities and support translanguaging for learning. Our conversations with you as you explore the topics we cover will evidence that it is possible for teachers to meet standards and create culturally responsive classrooms. We believe teachers must hold high expectations for ELs' academic achievement and make certain the ELs know they can achieve even while developing English. This requires that all lessons scaffold language using appropriate sheltered English, and that teachers continually investigate students' cultural capital (Daniel, Riley, & Kruger, chapter 6).

Examples of lessons showcase the types of language ELs need to explore to access and master conceptual foci in the different content areas. Selection and use of authentic and culturally relevant instructional materials is a must (Koss & Daniel, chapter 2). Texts that reflect ELs' rich cultural backgrounds will validate students' lives and experiences, applaud plurilingual identity development, and serve as bridges to comprehension. Learners will succeed academically when provided access to concepts through explicit and concrete language instruction.

Acquiring proficiency in an additional language means ELs also need purposeful writing instruction (Lee, chapter 3), and explicit teacher facilitation to develop writing skills across disciplines (Fang et al., chapter 5). Learning to write for different purposes is an arduous task that reminds me of the phrase *practice makes perfect*. The authors focus (1) on the strategies teachers need to incorporate in their lessons and (2) on the reasons that strategic instruction needs to be redefined for classrooms with ELs. Recommendations are based on prior research conducted by educators from K–12 to university levels.

Authors unanimously espouse the belief that to help ELs be college ready requires that K–12 teachers widen their instructional approaches and that teacher educators do their job well. We must all engage in a conscious and ongoing examination of learners' schooled and nonschooled cultural capital (Daniel, Riley, & Kruger, chapter 6). Identifying changes needed in the schoolhouse requires an awareness of the composition of EL populations and an examination of population trends and of what can be done better.

DEMOGRAPHIC REVELATIONS

Approximately 25 percent of students in U.S. schools speak a language other than English at home, with ELs composing 9 percent of all K–12 students enrolled in schools (OELA, 2015). This represents an increasing diversity across student populations that merits careful consideration.

According to the National Center for Education Statistics (2016), from 2003 through fall 2013, the number of white students enrolled in public elementary and secondary schools decreased from 28.4 to 25.2 million. In contrast, Hispanic students enrolled in schools during this period increased from 9 to 12.5 million, and the "percentage who were Hispanic increased from 19 to 25 percent" (NCES, 2016, p. 88). Projections for Hispanic student enrollment for 2025 reflect a probable increase to 29 percent of the total number of students.

School dropout rates calculated using data from the American Community Survey (ACS), which includes individuals living at home and those in institutional and noninstitutional group quarters, suggest there is work to be done in schools because all ELs are not achieving academically. Dropout rates in 2014 for Asians were lower in percentages (2.5 percent) than for whites (4.4) and higher for Pacific Islanders (10.6) and for Hispanics (10.7). Among the Asian category, some subgroups had startlingly higher dropout rates and others much lower rates: Burmese (27.5), Nepalese (19.6), Japanese (1.3), Chinese (1.2), and Korean (0.9).

An interesting comparison of youth born in the United States to those born in other countries reveals higher dropout rates for the latter: Hispanic (7.6 vs. 20.8), Asian (1.8 vs. 3.4), and Pacific Islander (7.1 to 23.4) (NCES, 2016, p. 196). It is evident that foreign-born students are not receiving sufficient support at levels K–12.

In my role as editor, I invited colleagues from across the country who I knew would write to what teachers need. Their words will encourage current and future teachers to experiment in their classrooms. They make suggestions for envisioning, developing, and implementing instructional methods that engage ELs, help students develop English, and focus on decreasing dropout rates.

REFERENCES

Kena, G., Hussar, W., McFarland, J., de Brey, C., Musu-Gillette, L., Wang, X., Zhang, J., Rathbun, A., Wilkinson-Flicker, S., Diliberti, M., Barmer, A., Bullock Mann, F., & Dunlop Velez, E. (2016). The Condition of educations 2016 (Report No.2016144). Washington, D.C.: National Center for Education Statistics, Institute of Education Sciences, Department of Education.

Office of English Language Acquisition (OELA). (2015). Profiles of English learners (ELs). (Fast Facts). Washington D.C.: U.S. Department of Education. Retrieved from http://www2.ed.gov/about/offices/list/oela/fast-facts/pel.pdf.

Acknowledgments

My appreciation to the authors who contributed their expertise to this project. Your commitment to the education of English learners is evident in your writing. Thanks for the great examples that you selected to share in your chapters! They perfectly illustrate a vision for how caring educators want to teach.

I thank Suzanne Canavan from Rowman & Littlefield for encouraging me to develop this book before her retirement.

And *muchísimas gracias* to my husband, *the noneducator*, for becoming knowledgeable about English learners and understanding my musings.

Foreword

The population of non-native English speakers has continued to grow dramatically over the first decade of the twenty-first century, as the United States (U.S.) has experienced dramatic demographic shifts in the cultural, linguistic and ethnic composition of the population. Because of this and many other reasons, today's mainstream classrooms increasingly include students for whom English is a second language. They are the most rapidly growing group of students in our nation's schools, and with a language barrier to participation and access in the education system they are also disproportionately underserved and underachieving. As teaching and learning is increasingly digitized, and our students interact as global citizens, it is imperative that we consider opportunities to assist learners from around the globe as they interact and communicate with others in networked learning spaces.

As our world becomes increasingly interconnected, the development of informed, literate members of the global community becomes ever more critical. As Internet connectivity becomes more ubiquitous around the globe, the next major influx of citizens to the web will be non-native English speakers. This transition is made even more complex as educators and students negotiate a world in which English is sometimes viewed as the lingua franca. The education of English language learners (ELs) is a matter of increasing urgency for the global community concerned about education and youth. Individual, personalized student-centered instruction from experts in the field is needed more now than ever before.

Given the significance of online informational text in schools and society, it is important to develop instructional opportunities designed to build the knowledge, skills, and dispositions needed by students as they connect from diverse cultures in a global classroom. As detailed in this book, the EL student population grows much faster than the overall student population, as non-native English speakers academic performance continues to lag behind their native speaker counterparts. Within this context, educators are seeking ways to engage ELs in the classroom. *English Learners at the Top of the Class: Reading and Writing for Authentic Purposes* helps fill that need by helping educators consider not only how to integrate ELs into the classroom and mainstream society, but also how to help them excel. I believe that our goal in these endeavors is to not only focus on the education of ELs, but to a greater extent empower all learners.

This book's chapters present the expertise of educators and researchers that serve on the front lines of educating youth. They know how to help ELs negotiate these spaces and practices. The authors encourage readers to utilize this text as partners in this experience by designing their own remixes of the materials in this text. Furthermore, this theme of empowerment is extended to these interactions with the reader as educators are encouraged to trust their instincts and make pedagogical decisions to help ELs succeed. Due to the incredible changes that are occurring as we move into a networked, plurilingual society, the authors provide a text can be used as a topographical map to help educators develop awareness of future ways to not only educate, but also empower ELs.

Together, the growing numbers of ELs, the persistent achievement gaps and barriers to access, and an increasingly high set of stakes add up to a seminal moment for people and institutions investing in the world's society. Fortunately, this is an era in which a strong research and practice base offers a consistent foundation to draw upon for solutions. In addition, there is a growing group of educators who are experienced in addressing the challenges facing ELs and the schools that serve them, and can offer the lens of their experiences, expertise and lessons learned. This book consolidates these areas of expertise and provides granular advice on preparing all students for success, regardless of where they live on the globe, or the language they speak.

—W. Ian O'Byrne

Introduction

Practicing teachers in the United States are flocking to universities to prepare to work with English learners (ELs). There are limits to the time educators are able to commit to rigorous courses after their school day is over, yet many do exactly this. They see in their schools that student populations are increasing in their cultural and linguistic diversity. They know that to reach these learners requires they develop a different skillset than their teacher preparation program may have presented.

Chapter authors bring to this book their experiences as teachers at levels K–12. Many of them learned English as a second language and experienced life as an EL in U.S. classrooms. They were all teachers who along the way began to work with ELs. Their engagement with culturally diverse students led them to become teacher educators. They are committed to preparing teachers who are energized to learn about their ELs' cultures and who want to make the schoolhouse a culturally responsive environment.

Teachers strive to learn how to communicate with their students when the classroom demographic has no common language. They need to identify ways to teach these learners through nonlinguistic pathways. Teachers also ask why some instructional strategies are purported to work with all students but need to be modified to address ELs' language needs.

Educators, regardless of the level they teach, often find that the language an entire class may have in common is the target language of study: English. What compounds the problem in planning curriculum is that in any given classroom students are at different levels of English language proficiency. Another issue is that learners' literacy experiences and their families' expectations for schooling may reflect the goals of the different educational systems in which they participated. Teachers need to clarify for families what expectations for students are in the U.S. system.

No educator can strive to have mastery of all the languages students use at home and in their communities. This is why the topics of the chapters you will read were selected: to address teachers' professional development needs.

SUPPORTING TEACHERS' PROFESSIONAL DEVELOPMENT

English Learners at the Top of the Class is a practice-oriented book that also contributes to the professional literature. It is written for teacher candidates and both new and experienced practicing teachers who want to design and deliver effective instructional paradigms across this country's diverse classrooms.

The information shared in this book is for the teacher who is reflective, is energetic, and believes in teachers being leaders in their school districts. It is for the educator who wants to share information that parents will understand. Proactive teachers who want to guide the steering wheel of their professional development might form an after-school book club, read one chapter of this text for each meeting of what may be called a "teacher advocacy group," discuss the reading at the first meeting, apply the information prior to the second meeting, and continue the process.

ORGANIZATION OF BOOK

The chapters in *English Learners at the Top of the Class* are organized into three parts:

Part I: Processes in Reading and Selection of Authentic Literature

This section is aimed at helping ELs understand text. It begins a conversation with the reader focused on increasing the focus on literacy in all content-area classes. This section informs parts 2 and 3, which center on ways for teachers to address disciplinary literacies.

Part 2: Disciplinary Literacies

Teachers want to foster English language acquisition in content-area classrooms and support ELs' pluriliteracies. In this section, the goal is to present ideas for authentic and *purposeful reading and writing instruction* that offers ELs opportunities for language learning every moment of the school day. Examples of classroom applications present concrete ways to extend and implement research-based pedagogy.

Part 3: Evaluation for Learning

The message in this section recursively joins the goal of helping ELs understand what they read, selection of culturally responsive materials, and the need for fair formative and summative assessments. The overarching message is that when teaching and evaluating ELs, teachers must ensure that the language in evaluations does not *skew test results*.

DESIGN AND CONTENT OF EACH CHAPTER

The chapters in this book are written with the goal of sharing information using the tone of a friendly conversation. The message in each chapter is accessible and useful to the reflective educator who wants to be able to effectively inform families about schooling expectations in this country.

Components of Each Chapter

1. The *initial presentation* of the topic to be discussed is found in a few sentences before each chapter's narrative begins. This offers the reader a quick glimpse of what the chapter author will cover.
2. The second section introduces the reader to the *rationale or conceptual framework* that supports the recommendations for practice that will be shared in section 3. Chapter authors present their arguments for strategies that teachers might follow to plan instruction in classrooms with ELs. The objective of this section is to provide information that will support teachers' curricular innovations.
3. The next section offers *practical applications for the classroom*. It is here that the writers focus on identifying and presenting examples of the lesson components that are needed to design culturally responsive instruction.
4. Then a *recommendations* section presents additional options for planning classroom instruction that teachers may want to investigate.
5. The last section, a list of *resources*, is developed by each author as best fits the topic of each chapter. Some writers shared resources for teachers, others technology resources, and yet others listed both suggestions for materials to use in lesson planning and examples of up-to-date current technologies.

I

Processes in Reading and Selection of Authentic Literature

Chapter One

What Teachers of ELs Need to Consider Regarding Nonverbal Processes in Reading Comprehension

Fabiola P. Ehlers-Zavala

The author shares her commitment to the education of English learners in a discussion of ways to provide students paths to creating nonverbal imagery during reading processes. Using concrete examples, she applies Paivio's dual coding theory as a key theoretical foundation that can lead teachers and students to better understand and facilitate reading comprehension in the second language learner.

Reading comprehension is about making sense of the texts people read, and this activity "has always been multimodal" (Rowsell et al., 2013, p. 1182). Therefore, it would seem only natural that a theory of literacy would have to be one that allows us to account for this experience. In this conversation, Paivio's dual coding theory (DCT) is embraced as the theoretical foundation for more fully understanding the reading comprehension processes of English learners (ELs). His theory allows us to understand the multimodal experience embodied in reading comprehension.

Why should DCT be considered to understand and describe ELs' reading comprehension?

To date, after working with ELs across many educational contexts, the author continues to belief that Paivio's DCT is the most appropriate theory to fully make sense of literacy development not only in the first but also in a second or foreign language with ELs of all ages (Ehlers-Zavala, 1999, 2005, 2014, 2015; Ehlers-Zavala & Maciejewski, 2016). Sadoski and Paivio (2001, 2013) fully articulated how DCT can serve as a unified theory of literacy.

An extension of DCT, which had been introduced to the field in 1971, was Paivio and Desrochers's 1980 model of DCT for the bilingual mind. Similar to the arguments that Sadoski and Paivio (2001, 2013) offered for DCT as a theory to understand literacy, the DCT model for the bilingual model gives us the tool to understand second/foreign language literacy development as well as learner or reader performance on comprehension tasks. Mental imagery, engagement, and affect are key to understanding cognition and reading comprehension.

In essence, as Sadoski and Paivio (2013) describe, "DCT is about the nature of two great symbolic systems of cognition: language and mental imagery" (p. ix). These two systems function and interact in three distinct ways or levels. The most basic one is the representational level. At this level, during cognition, external input (such as words contained in a text) are encoded into verbal units (logogens) or nonverbal units (imagens).

At another level, the associationist, the systems may trigger the action of other types of internal activity within each of them. That is, one word may trigger another word; one mental image may trigger the formation of another mental image.

Finally, at a referential level, there may be cognitive activity that activates cognitive action in the other system (crossover functioning). For instance, a word may trigger the formation of a mental image and vice versa. This type of functional activity is incredibly flexible and dynamic, and, therefore, it can accommodate both individual and cultural differences easily.

These characteristics of the theory allow readers to understand how the literacy development of learners can be so incredibly unique to the individual, and at the same time, be mediated by the cultural and social background of the reader. As Sadoski and Paivio stated (2004), DCT does not rely on abstract or propositional models (e.g., schema theory) to account for comprehension. DCT is scientific in nature (as widely demonstrated across numerous investigations), cognitive, associationist, embodied in real human experience, constructivist, and therefore well positioned to account for what literacy processes seem to entail (Sadoski & Paivio, 2013, pp. 1–7).

Finally, the DCT model for the bilingual learner assumes the existence of multiple verbal systems, which can connect to each other directly or indirectly via one common nonverbal system (the imagery system). As a bilingual/bicultural individual, this makes intuitive sense, but whether readers have multiple verbal systems or just one certainly requires further research. What cannot be denied, however, is that when reading, the nonverbal experience (whether it is in the form of mental images or affective responses to a text) is likely to be present. Thus, DCT remains a viable theory for understanding and explaining what happens when reading.

PRACTICAL APPLICATIONS OF DCT: IMPLICATIONS FOR UNIMODAL, BIMODAL, AND MULTIMODAL TEXTS

When thinking about the nature of texts, whether fiction or nonfiction, there is a wide range of textual materials to consider. Some texts may be purely verbal or nonverbal in nature, known as unimodal texts (a nonillustrated story would be an example of a unimodal text; a wordless picture book would be another); others may involve both verbal and nonverbal elements, known as bimodal texts (such as picture books or illustrated texts that contain both verbal and nonverbal elements). In these types of texts, the verbal and nonverbal elements may be presented in concert with each other in a variety of ways.

Yet other texts will introduce readers to a world of possibilities through the use of multimedia such as sound and interactivity of various kinds that are possible through technology. These texts are known as multimodal texts. Thus, effectively comprehending a text also requires that the reader learn to effectively work with different types of reading materials. In light of all this, diverse types of texts will posit different demands on readers when it comes to reading comprehension.

Comprehending Unimodal Texts

As previously defined, unimodal texts are those that are exclusively verbal or exclusively nonverbal. Exclusively verbal texts are those that are not accompanied by any other supporting elements, such as illustrations, photographs, tables, charts, and so forth. When ELs encounter reading materials that do not contain any additional elements outside the verbal, they must focus and rely exclusively on the verbal nature of those texts. Through sensory analysis as they interact with the texts, ELs will work on encoding the text in a verbal and/or nonverbal modality.

In order to illustrate the concept just described, let us consider the following text (please, read the following micro-text silently): "South America has produced many famous artists, novelists, filmmakers, and poets. Chilean poets Pablo Neruda and Gabriela Mistral both were awarded the Nobel Prize for their work. Neruda wrote about everyday objects, including rain, tomatoes, and socks. Mistral wrote for and about children" (*Latin America*, 2003, p. 75).

Now ask yourself the following questions:

- Did this passage elicit any mental images?
- How did this passage make me feel? Engaged or not?

Of course, when it comes to these questions, there are no right or wrong answers. Answers will vary, and they will likely depend on how much background a particular reader brought into the reading experience. For someone who can relate to these two authors, Neruda and Mistral, in very precise and particular ways, the level of imagery formation, personal engagement, and understanding of this text is likely very high. A Chilean reader, in reading that excerpt, would likely experience a sense of personal pride about these two authors being mentioned in a U.S. textbook. It is possible that if that reader had an opportunity to visit the three homes of Neruda in Chile, those images may have come to that reader's mind.

But of course, for a reader who has not experienced all of what was described above, the number of images may be far fewer and possibly less rich. Such a reader may comprehend the verbal aspect of the text, but the overall reading experience may be less engaging and perhaps less memorable into the future.

In other words, individual and contextual/situational factors will likely mediate the levels of activation of the verbal and the nonverbal systems in the comprehension of a particular text. When readers interact with texts, instructional factors aside, their experience is also mediated by individual and sociocultural factors that will shape the mental reading/comprehension experience. After all, comprehending a text is about making meaning, and making meaning is "always relative to social practices" (Ivarsson, Linderoth, & Säljö, 2009, p. 210).

Likewise, unimodal texts can also be purely nonverbal. This is the case of wordless picture books as well as comic books, which lack a verbal narration and, instead, offer a visual narrative. That is, when readers interact with these texts, they (whether alone or in interaction with others) are left to create the verbal story as they engage in the sensory analysis of the images contained in that text. So a purely visual text is likely to be encoded and stored not only around pictorial representations in the mind, but also in terms of verbal images, depending on where the ELs find themselves in terms of literacy processes.

Consider, for instance, the wordless book by Suzy Lee (2008) titled *Wave*. This book is a delightful representation of a little girl's day at the beach. In turning over the pages, for a reader who grew up on the coast, regardless of age, it is likely that the passage evoked vivid mental images of former experiences on the beach, watching the waves, looking at the seagulls fly or land on the sand. It is possible that such reader can almost hear the ocean waves splashing against the rocks.

Comprehending Bimodal Texts

Bimodal texts are texts accompanied by a visual modality that, according to researchers, may play "just as important a role as the verbal in creating meaning and shaping readers" (Painter, Martin, & Unsworth, 2013, p. 2). At times, bimodal texts are less understood when it comes to how the image works in interaction with the verbal (Painter, Martin & Unsworth, 2013). Examples of bimodal texts are picture books—those that contain both pictures and texts.

When reading bimodal texts, "both words and pictures confront our eyes, and consequently they have literal relationships as well as symbolic ones. The words of a text are not just symbols of spoken sounds but part of the visual pattern of the page, without reference to their actual meaning" (Nodelman, 1988, p. 53).

Some picture books, for example, show a very complex relationship between pictures and texts, as Bateman (2014) indicated when referring to examples from the very well-known picture book by Sendak (1965) titled *Where the Wild Things Are*. Bateman points to the double-spread page that shows Max leaving the Wild Things as an example of this complexity, which does not fully depict all that is conveyed in the verbal text. Thus, readers are expected to integrate all of the elements to achieve full comprehension of the story being told.

Bateman (2014) offered the following observation: "As some authors have suggested, therefore, the picture book will tend to pick out of the stream of the narrative particular highpoints or key moments for which a visual rendition can be productively given" (p. 78). It is up to the readers, therefore, to make the full connection between the verbal and the nonverbal.

Yet, in other books, the relationship will be clearer. Consider, for example, the more straightforward classic picture book by Beatrix Potter, *The Tale of Peter Rabbit*. As readers explore this book, there seems to be a very clear depiction of the words contained in the verbal text captured in the pictorial illustrations that accompany the text.

The implications for ELs who are in the process of becoming proficient language users and effective readers are important to consider. Less proficient ELs may over-rely on the nonverbal elements contained in a book that accompany the verbal. This may account for the diversity in results derived from research that may on the surface appear contradictory when it comes to assessing the usefulness of illustrations that accompany texts. For this reason, it is imperative that teachers of ELs be aware of the need to help them learn to carefully examine the role of pictures or illustrations in a text.

In other words, teachers need to help ELs in understanding the pictorial rhetoric and what different elements in a picture may convey in terms of meaning. For ELs who struggle, this may be a critical element in learning to become effective readers.

Comprehending Multimodal Texts

Though "there is a long history of creating online digital resources to support and promote young children's reading skills through the implementation of computerized methods, from CD-ROMs to alternative web-based technologies" (Underwood & Farrington-Flint, 2015, p. 47), the ELs of the new millennium, or e-generation, are increasingly exposed to multimodal texts, as they are highly likely to interact with the multiplicity of e-devices available (e.g., iPads, iPods, and other touchscreen tablet devices).

Nowadays, increasingly more so, ELs around the globe encounter texts that combine an interesting juxtaposition of semiotic systems that go beyond the visual. An online text, for example, may give ELs the opportunity to hear the text as they interact with it. Basically, as Richards (2009) noted, "Now schools have the computers (with graphics) and they are connected to a vast internet resources" (p. 334). But, of course, in some contexts, these resources are inevitably linked to the socioeconomics of school districts. There is still a significant access gap related to socioeconomic status tied to the social conditions of families (Cummins, 2008).

Yet, despite the world of possibilities, this is still a territory that represents a challenge for ELs. A question can be certainly raised as to whether or not teachers are technologically prepared to make the most of what is now available to ensure the educational success of ELs. There are some who still question whether there is enough evidence to endorse the use of multimedia as an effective tool in the learning experience of ELs, given the limited research available (Cummins, 2008).

Underwood and Farrington-Flint (2015) questioned whether e-books, for example, are effective or serve as mere "adjunct" to real reading experiences. But, in citing others, they also acknowledge the appeal that e-story books have on young readers and reiterate the possible benefits other researchers have identified, as e-books allow young readers to:

- enjoy a text as they interact with events and characters on screen
- read for meaning and enjoy stories with focused talk and joint attention supported by the explicit nature of the text on the screen
- develop their understanding of print through text which is highlighted as it is read
- develop their own narratives linked to what is happening on screen
- understand aspects of texts on screen, such as icons, navigational features and "hotspots"

- develop ICT [informal computer technological] skills such as use of the mouse
- collaborate and negotiate with others. (p. 49)

In fact, Underwood and Farrington-Flint (2015) further reminded us that

> the term "edutainment" has been used to characterize the highly interactive playful qualities and educational goals associated with online resources to help students acquire some of the core skills associated with reading, writing and comprehension (Underwood & Underwood, 1990). It is this combination of education with engaging multimedia qualities that enthuse and engage learners of all ages. (p. 49)

In today's world, therefore, it is well known that ELs of all ages will likely experience reading in a multimodal fashion, and it is that experience in itself that needs to be recognized and explained in any theory that intends to account for reading comprehension. In this context, it is evident that DCT offers teachers an opportunity to begin to understand the multiplicity of mental experiences that the act of reading can evoke.

In short, whether ELs encounter unimodal, bimodal, or multimodal texts, it is highly possible that they will experience the process of reading comprehension in a multiplicity of ways, activating both verbal and nonverbal processes spontaneously. This concept must be fully explored by classroom teachers to adequately understand the experiences of ELs as readers. Attending to the nonverbal processes may shed a significant level of understanding to guide ELs on how to gain control of the cognitive and metacognitive strategies needed for successful reading.

After all, as Grabe (2009) pointed out, effective readers are engaged readers who automatically/spontaneously engage in a number of activities:

1. They read selectively according to goals.
2. They read carefully in key places.
3. They reread as appropriate.
4. They monitor their reading continuously, and they are aware of whether or not they comprehend the text.
5. They identify important information.
6. They try to fill in gaps in the text through inferences and prior knowledge.
7. They make guesses about unknown words.
8. They use text-structure information to guide understanding.
9. They make inferences about the author, key information, and main ideas.
10. They attempt to integrate ideas from different parts of the text.
11. They build interpretations of the text as they read.

12. They build main-idea summaries.
13. They evaluate the text and the author and, as a result, form feelings about the text.
14. They attempt to resolve difficulties. (p. 228)

It is therefore imperative that teachers of ELs attend to ELs' academic needs in all aspects involved in reading comprehension and address the various elements that may be part of textual production. The nonverbal elements of a text can be as important as the verbal elements in successful comprehension of diverse materials. The internal mental processes must be scrutinized, and ELs need to be aware of how critically important it is to monitor and control these.

RECOMMENDATIONS FOR ACTIONS AND RESOURCES

In light of this discussion, below are five key recommendations for all teachers to consider when preparing to assist ELs in strengthening their reading skills:

1. Seek and maintain ongoing professional development in the areas of reading comprehension research as well as the use of technology. This action is key given that there is yet much to be discovered and understood about the influence of nonverbal processes in reading, the role of illustrations and other elements accompanying texts, and the effects of technology in mediating reading comprehension as experienced by L2 readers.

2. Define and model mental imagery for your ELs. Start by using very simple and concrete examples. You may use one-word texts or simple sentences that are concrete and can evoke a mental image. You can write that example on the board or display it for ELs to see in another way. Have them read the example provided silently, and then offer an account of what you experienced when you saw that example. Then invite ELs to share their account. Continue to scaffold understanding by using short texts of increasing length and invite students to offer their accounts.

As texts increase in length and complexity, do not be surprised if you start realizing that the reports your ELs provide may at time deviate from the printed texts. That is often the case when students are in the process of learning English and are not fully proficient. They may end up creating other stories in their minds. Activities of this sort will allow you to check whether or not your students are on track and able to comprehend the texts.

3. Continuously assess ELs' ability to engage the nonverbal when reading. Once your ELs have understood the concept of mental imagery, systematically or periodically invite them to report back to you orally and/or in writing if they have experienced any mental images (or affective responses (if appropriate) while reading the textual materials you incorporate in your teaching. You may also provide them with a four-point rating scale that allows them to indicate whether or not they experienced lots of mental images (4) or no mental images (1).

The same can be done to assess their emotional responses to the materials they read to gauge their levels of textual engagement.

4. Develop a repertoire of strategies to engage the nonverbal when reading. Regardless of the types of texts your ELs encounter, ensure they know how to engage their nonverbal process before, during, and after reading. As you help ELs implement a variety of reading strategies to prepare to read a text, you can have them visualize what a story or text may be about.

You can also have them provide an account of mental processes as they read and interact with a text, and you may have them review this account after reading by having them go back to the sections in the text that would connect to the mental images they experienced.

When working with texts that are accompanied by visual elements, have ELs examine those elements and critically think about how they connect to the verbal text they are reading. This way, learners can increase their attention to the texts they read and learn the benefits of attending to other elements that may contribute to the meaning of a particular text. Struggling readers often ignore all of these additional support systems.

5. Exercise a critical eye in selecting reading materials. Ensure that each time you select a bimodal text, in particular, you are comfortable articulating how the visual choices contained in that particular text relate to the "structural and verbal components of the narrative text" (Painter, Martin, & Unsworth, 2013, p. 2).

Considering Bateman's classification of images (2014), ask yourself the following questions: What types of images are these? Are they graphic (pictures, status, designs)? Are they optical (mirrors or projections)? Are they perceptual (sense data, "species," appearances)? Are they mental (dreams, memories, ideas, fantasmata)? Are they verbal (metaphors, descriptions)?

Further, consider these questions: Are these images mirroring the verbal text? Are they complimentary? Are they expanding the information contained in a text? Could they be sending the reader in a completely different direction when it comes to reading comprehension? Are these images in possible contradiction to the verbal element contained in this text?

RELEVANT RESOURCES

Below you will find some professional readings teachers of ELs may find useful in preparing to work with ELs and help them strengthen their ability to become better readers.

- Bateman, J. (2014). *Text and image: A critical introduction to the visual/verbal divide*. New York, NY: Routledge. This book is an excellent resource that provides a well-grounded introduction to the text and image connection, as suggested by its title. Of particular interest is chapter 4, which introduces the concept of visual narrative and describes the different ways in which texts and images can relate to one another in picture books.
- Hull, G., Stornaiuolo, A., & Sterponi, A. (2013). Imagined readers and hospitable texts: Global youths connect online. In D. E. Alvermann, N. J. Unrau, and R. B. Ruddell (Eds.), *Theoretical models and processes of reading* (pp. 1208–1240). Newark, DE: International Reading Association. This is a chapter that discusses the demands of reading online, and reports on research conducted with youth in four different countries over the course of three years (India, United States, South Africa, and Norway). It also covers text production using multimedia.
- Langer de Ramirez, L. (2010). *Empower English language learners with tools from the web*. Thousand Oaks, CA: Corwin Press. This practical book offers teachers many suggestions for online or web-based resources that can be considered when helping learners develop specific skills as they interact with multimodal texts.
- Nodelman, P. (1988). *Words about pictures*. Athens, GA: The University of Georgia Press. This is a classic book that guides readers into the basics of picture books. It is a must read when it comes to children's literature.
- Roswell, J., Pahl, K., & Street, B. (2013). The social practice of multimodal reading: A new literacy studies—Multimodal perspective on reading. In D. E. Alvermann, N. J. Unrau, and R. B. Ruddell (Eds.), *Theoretical models and processes of reading* (pp. 1182–1207). Newark, DE: International Reading Association. This chapter offers readers an introduction to reading in the multimodal era, as situated within two orientations: New literacy studies and multimodality research, highlighting the new demands on reading nowadays.
- Zeigler, L. L. & Johns, J. L. (2004). *Visualization. Using mental images to strengthen comprehension*. Dubuque, IA: Kendall/Hunt. This is a great practical resource for teachers that offers strategies, rubrics, and assessments to help learners develop or strengthen their ability to visualize texts.

CONCLUSION

ELs are individuals who bring a quantitative and qualitative diverse array of experiences in both their primary and second or foreign language to the reading experience. Those experiences, however, do not always neatly or perfectly align with the texts they read. It is highly probable that, when reading, ELs evoke or activate both verbal and/or nonverbal mental processes prior to, during, and after reading.

The personal elicitation of these mental processes mentioned above is directly connected to the types of texts they read and their own experiences (sociocultural and linguistic resources). Therefore, a teacher's task is to help ELs uncover and more fully understand what resources ELs possess so that they (ELs) can gain control and mastery over them in a very concerted and purposeful way. A teacher's task is also to develop an understanding for what cross-cultural influences may be positively or negatively influencing the reading comprehension experience of the ELs.

All in all, teachers need to engage in the explicit exploration and teaching of what ELs as readers are going through when interacting with texts.

REFERENCES

Alvermann, D. E., Unrau, N. J., & Ruddell, R. B. (2013). *Theoretical models and processes of reading* (6th ed.). Newark, DE: International Reading Association.

Bateman, J. A. (2014). *Text and image. A critical introduction to the visual/verbal divide*. New York, NY: Routledge.

Cummins, J. (2008). Technology, literacy, and young second language learners. In L. Lean Parker (Ed.), *Technology-mediated learning environments for young English learners* (pp. 61–98). New York, NY: Lawrence Erlbaum Associates.

Ehlers-Zavala, F. (1999). *Reading an illustrated and non-illustrated story: Dual coding in the foreign language classroom* (Doctoral dissertation, Illinois State University, 1999). Dissertation Abstracts International, 60, 2887.

Ehlers-Zavala, F. (2005). Bilingual reading from a dual coding perspective. In J. Cohen, K. T. McAlister, K. Rolstad, & J. MacSwan (Eds.), *ISB4: Proceedings of the 4th International Symposium on Bilingualism* (pp. 656–662). Somerville, MA: Cascadilla Press.

Ehlers-Zavala, F. (2014). *Dual coding theory (DCT) for the bilingual mind as a theory of L2 reading/writing*. Poster presentation delivered at the 17th World Congress of the International Association of Applied Linguistics (AILA), Brisbane, Australia.

Ehlers-Zavala, F. (2015). *Meeting the reading comprehension challenges of diverse English language learners in K–12. Key contributions from reading research*. Paper presented at the annual meeting of the International Literacy Association (ILA), Saint Louis, MO.

Ehlers-Zavala, F., & Maciejewski, A. (2016). *Mental imagery experienced by both pathway and non-pathway graduate students in an engineering course at a US Research I institution*. Paper presented at the annual meeting of the American Association for Applied Linguistics (AAAL), Orlando, FL.

Grabe, W. (2009). *Reading in a second language. Moving from theory to practice*. New York, NY: Cambridge University Press.

Ivarsson, J., Linderoth, J., & Säljö, R. (2009). Representations in practices: A socio-cultural approach to multimodality in reasoning. In C. Jewitt (Ed.), *The Routledge handbook of multimodal analysis* (pp. 201–212). New York, NY: Routledge.

Langer de Ramirez, L. (2010). *Empower English language learners with tools from the web*. Thousand Oaks, CA: Corwin Press.

Jacobs, H. H., Randolph, B., & LeVasseur, M. (2003). *Latin America*. Glenview, IL: Prentice Hall.

Lee, S. (2008). *Wave*. San Francisco, CA: Chronicle Books.

Nodelman, P. (1988). *Words about pictures*. Athens, GA: The University of Georgia Press.

Painter, C., Martin, J. R., & Unsworth, L. (2013). *Reading visual narratives*. Bristol, CT: Equinox.

Paivio, A. (1971). *Imagery and verbal processes.* New York, NY: Holt, Reinhart, & Winston.
Paivio, A. (1990). *Mental representations. A dual coding approach.* New York, NY: Oxford University Press.
Paivio, A., & Desrochers, A. (1980). A dual coding approach to bilingual memory. *Canadian Journal of Psychology, 34,* 388–399.
Potter, B. (1972). *The tale of Peter Rabbit.* New York, NY: Dover.
Richards, G. (2009). Book review: Technology-mediated learning environments for young English learners. *Educational Technology & Society, 12*(2), 334–336.
Rowsell, J., Kress, J., Pahl, K., & Street, B. (2013). The social practice of multimodal reading: A new literacy studies—multimodal perspective on reading. In R. B. Ruddell and N. J. Unrau (Eds.), *Theoretical models and processes of reading* (5th ed., pp. 1182–1207). Newark, DE: International Reading Association.
Sadoski, M., & Paivio, A. (2001). *Imagery and text: A dual coding theory of reading and writing.* Mahwah, NJ: Lawrence Erlbaum Associates.
Sadoski, M., & Paivio, A. (2004). A dual coding theoretical model of reading. In R. B. Ruddell and N. J. Unrau (Eds.), *Theoretical models and processes of reading* (5th ed., pp. 1329–1362). Newark, DE: International Reading Association.
Sadoski, M., & Paivio, A. (2013). *Imagery and text: A dual coding theory of reading and writing* (2nd ed.). New York, NY: Routledge.
Sadoski, M., Paivio, A., & Goetz, E. T. (1991). A critique to schema theory in reading and a dual coding alternative. *Reading Research Quarterly, 26*(4), 251–271.
Sendak, M. (2012). *Where the wild things are.* New York, NY: HarperCollins.
Underwood, J. D. M., & Farrington-Flint, L. (2015). *Learning and the E-Generation.* Malden, MA: Wiley-Blackwell.
Underwood, J. D. M., & Underwood, G. (1990). Computers and learning: Helping children acquire thinking skills. Oxford, UK: Blackwell.
Zeigler, L. L., & John, J. L. (2005). *Visualization: Using mental images to strengthen comprehension.* Dubuque, IA: Kendall Hunt.

Chapter Two

Culturally Relevant Literature for Multilingual Classrooms

Melanie Koss and Mayra C. Daniel

When teachers explore the contribution of authentic literature to the classroom, they are fascinated by how the appropriate selection of books can revolutionize the schoolhouse. The authors encourage thoughtful examination of books to ensure these provide clear windows and revealing mirrors that aid students' understandings of diverse cultures and experiences.

As U.S. classrooms become more diverse, issues of identity, language, and cultural competence are coming to the forefront of pedagogy and educational research. Research shows that English learners (ELs) possess significant cultural knowledge and skills that can be capitalized on in the classroom, yet these skills are often not utilized in effective ways. Too often, ELs' rich cultural backgrounds and non-schooling experiences are treated as barriers and deficits rather than as means to academic success.

As teacher educators, these authors believe in making classrooms welcoming by valuing all learners' lives and experiences. Tapping in to ELs' "funds of knowledge" (González, Moll, & Amanti, 2005) sends a signal to students that their experiences and lives are meaningful and valued. An effective means of incorporating students' funds of knowledge in the classroom is through the use of culturally diverse, relevant, and authentic children's literature.

Children's literature conveys cultural messages and societal values that help children learn about who they are and where they fit into their wider world. When teachers provide students with a broad array of literature that includes diverse characters and perspectives in stories, they offer all students visions of self and of others.

As noted by Bishop (1990), children's literature provides learners with an entry point to see themselves and others in books, and as such, opens opportunities to discuss the similarities, differences, and varieties of cultures in the world. She posited that children need to see themselves reflected in literature (i.e., look into a mirror), to see the lives of others (i.e., look into a window), and also see themselves being able to transverse between groups and worlds (i.e., passing through a sliding glass door) (Bishop, 1992). Diverse literature opens avenues of discussion (Colby & Lyon, 2004).

"By including an abundance of literature depicting diverse perspectives, teachers open doors to awareness and understanding" (Landt, 2011, p. 1). However, teachers need to do more than simply include diverse literature into their classrooms and curricula. They need to incorporate such literature in strategic ways, capitalizing on not only students' diverse cultural backgrounds but also their dynamic plurilingualism.

These authors believe in a need for culturally responsive classrooms that integrate culturally relevant children's literature to foster students' reading motivation thus enhancing their cultural competence, their pride in their plurilingualism, and their literacy skills. What follows is a discussion of culturally responsive classrooms, culturally relevant literature and its importance to ELs, and three ways to authentically use literature that is culturally authentic and relevant in the classroom.

THE CULTURALLY RESPONSIVE SCHOOLHOUSE

Culturally responsive pedagogy validates all students' languages and cultures and considers them a valuable asset to the learning environment (Dixson & Fasching-Varner, 2009; Gay, 2002; TESOL, 2009). "Culturally responsive classrooms specifically acknowledge the presence of culturally diverse students and the need for these students to find relevant connections among themselves and with the subject matter and the tasks teachers ask them to perform" (Montgomery, 2001, p. 4). It acknowledges and values the idea that an individual's background influences and impacts his or her learning and posits that it is helpful to begin to construct meaning using the funds of knowledge as a starting point.

One of the best ways to increase literacy is for students to read for enjoyment (Brown, 2007; Guthrie & Wigfield, 2000). Educators play a crucial role in developing students' attitudes toward reading and influencing their levels of motivation to read (Kelley, Wilson, & Koss, 2012; Ryan & Patrick, 2001; Taylor, Pearson, Peterson, & Rodriguez, 2003).

Students who are positively motivated to read are more likely to engage in reading activities because they believe in their abilities to succeed with the skills they possess (Guthrie et al., 2004). Engaged readers are confident, are metacognitively aware, and understand how reading impacts learning. They are motivated to read by personal goals and interests, knowledgeable regarding what they read, and strategic when comprehending (Guthrie, McGough, Bennett, & Rice, 1996).

Thus, fostering reading motivation is critical for ELs (Cummins, 2003) who are reading not only for enjoyment but also to learn the English language. Exposing ELs to books that interest them and connect to their lives and needs will motivate them to read. ELs see reading as relevant when the characters and context of the stories provide a medium to compare or contrast their communities to those presented in the books.

A common challenge for ELs is that they are often presented literary texts that have unfamiliar topics and do not value or capitalize on their cultural norms in the school setting (Peregoy & Boyle, 2013). Classrooms that integrate use of culturally authentic texts encourage students to construct meaning, and influence their literacy practices to create engaged learners. Using authentic literature relevant to students' lives and cultures allows them to make connections between there in- and out-of-school literacies (Larson & Marsh, 2005), promote cultural competence, and provide a global perspective of the world (Au, 2001; Dixson & Fasching-Varner, 2009; Howard, 2003; Morrison, Robbins, & Rose, 2008). Its use also increases students' academic achievement (Gay, 2002; Lohfink, 2010; Morrison et al., 2008; Souto-Manning, 2009).

CULTURALLY RELEVANT LITERATURE AND ITS IMPORTANCE FOR ELS

Culturally relevant literature, also referred to as culturally specific or culturally pluralistic literature, is literature that accurately depicts and captures elements of a culture. Although every person's life and experience of their culture is unique, and one book cannot represent the minutia of an entire culture, a combination of cultural snapshots can yield glimpses into components of a culture that, put together, can provide an understanding of the lives of others and increase the chance that ELs will see themselves in books.

Depictions of diverse populations must be authentic and relevant to a story. The cultural descriptors of the characters matter; they cannot simply be included as tokens, but the cultural knowledge must play a critical role in the story and support a culturally conscious ideology (Gray, 2009; Martinez, Koss, & Johnson, 2016; McNair, 2010; Yoon, Simpson, & Haag, 2010). There are many things to consider when evaluating a book for its cultural relevancy.

Culturally relevant books of high quality portray a culture realistically, authentically, and present ideologies that are culturally conscious. Real-life descriptions and images of characters should be present, and the characters should be involved in realistic, relatable plots. These books do not confirm or depict stereotypes, but rather allow students to see themselves and their lives in accurate ways (Ching, 2005; Gray, 2009). Culturally relevant books should include accurate and authentic language conventions, images, cultural information, and cultural experiences. Also, story elements true to a culture's beliefs and traditions that support biculturalism and biliteracy should be included in the curriculum (Ching, 2005; McNair, 2010; Yoon et al., 2010). In addition, quality culturally relevant books can represent characters recognizing and accepting aspects of U.S. culture. However, it is critical that this does not supersede characters retaining and maintaining pride in their culture of origin. Thus, the inclusion of culturally relevant literature in an educational setting is of vital importance for ELs. When presented with literature in which they see their families and cultural norms depicted, ELs grasp how their cultures and languages contribute to greater society, thus eliminating issues of cultural mismatch (Cummins, 2009).

Gay (2000) posits that the curriculum for culturally diverse students must be inclusive and portray their realities. As classrooms are becoming increasingly diverse and multilingual (U.S. Census Bureau, 2013), having diverse populations represented in the literature teachers bring into the classroom will help ELs become more engaged with their own learning and enhance their literacy skills (Gangi, 2008; Hughes-Hassel, Barkley, & Koehler, 2009; TESOL, 2009). Seeing oneself in characters and connecting to them—looking into a mirror—encourages students to read (Heflin & Barksdale-Ladd, 2001). When students identify with the characters and situations found in text and illustrations, their level of reading enjoyment increases, leading to increased reading overall (DeLeón, 2002).

THREE WAYS TO USE CULTURALLY RELEVANT LITERATURE AUTHENTICALLY

We have discussed the importance of culturally responsive classrooms and culturally relevant literature. Next, we present three ways educators can consciously integrate culturally relevant literature into their classrooms to capitalize on their students' funds of knowledge. We take a look at how culturally relevant literature can be used as a multicultural lens to build confident learners, as a multilingual lens to recognize the worth of all languages, and as a strategic lens to raise metacognitive awareness.

Using Literature to Explore Multicultural Awareness

The most common way multicultural literature is integrated into classrooms is through a multicultural lens. This lens allows students to see themselves and others in literature and is based on exploring similarities and differences among cultures. It provides teachers a way to offer students an accurate view of today's world and a bridge to help them link the multicultural realities of the world with their classroom space and community.

Bridging identities across world cultures requires the classroom environment give ELs and their teachers a multicultural lens that empowers them to value difference. This lens recognizes and builds on students' cultural capital and embraces the idea that students' knowledge base extends beyond their formal schooling to include their non-schooling knowledge (Bourdieu, 1987; González, Moll, & Amanti, 2005). Using culturally relevant literature provides a springboard for ELs to understand where their knowledge base fits into their classrooms and their world (TESOL, 2009).

Careful thought should be given to book selection. Take a step back and look at the books you are choosing to include in your classroom library and curriculum. Do the books in your collection:

- provide a balanced mix of "mirror," "window," and "sliding glass door" books?
- help build an understanding of diverse cultures and experiences?
- include stories of diverse linguistic populations?
- include bi-, tri-, or plurilingual titles?
- include books by authors and illustrators of diverse cultural and linguistic backgrounds?
- reflect or deny the attitudes of the adults in my students' communities?
- include narrative and illustrations that portray feelings of cultural superiority or inferiority in their presentation of the learners' communities and families?

You may wish to refer to the Council for Interracial Books for Children's (1974) *10 Quick Ways to Analyze Children's Books for Racism and Sexism* article as a guide for evaluating titles of interest.

Rosenblatt (1978) discusses the importance of the transactions individuals have with the texts they read. Learners will each bring something different to a text, so as they read, students engage in negotiations that require they compare their world to the world(s) they see in books. Their personal backgrounds impact their understanding of text as well as the information they take away from it. No two people read and interpret a text the same way.

We want ELs learning a new language and culture to identify similarities and differences within a book and compare the norms of their home culture to the one presented by the author. After this, as students work to grasp the meaning(s) presented within the author's words and, if relevant, examine the illustrations in the book, they come to understand how their interpretations lead them to new conclusions and questions about the way human beings live and interact with one another. In facilitating classroom conversations, you may need to step away from your personal cultural views and allow students to take a more active role in guiding the discussion.

Classroom Conversations That Build Confidence

One way ELs' curiosity about the world is fostered is when they are exposed to books that relate to immigrant experiences. These may include a focus on familial struggles with language, hardships due to economic survival and border crossings, and mismatches experienced in the processes that surround adjusting to life in a new country. ELs need to see that their experiences are similar to those of classmates so that they do not feel they, alone, have felt the loneliness of being *the other*. Select books for your classrooms that allow the students to identify:

- the strengths within their families of origin;
- the similarities and differences across their families and the communities they see reflected in the books; and
- the ways different diverse communities interact.

See textbox 2.1 for an annotated bibliography of books that can be used in the classroom to foster discussions relating to adjusting to life in a new country.

Literature That Explores Immigrant Journeys and Experiences

Buitrago, J. (2015). *Two white rabbits*. Toronto, CA: Groundwood. (Gr. K–3)
A young girl and her father face many challenges as they make their way to the U.S. border from Central America in search of a new life. They travel by foot, by catching rides with others, and primarily on the roof of a train, stopping when detained or in need of money. The story is told from the perspective of the girl, who doesn't know the truth behind where they are going but who feels safe because she is with her father and her two white rabbits.

Danticat, E. (2015). *Mama's nightingale: A story of immigration and separation*. New York, NY: Dial. (Gr. 2–5)
Saya's Haitian mother was sent to an immigration center for undocumented immigrants, and her father's repeated attempts to free her by writing letters to judges, congressmen, newspapers, and TV stations are not successful. In order to maintain connection with her daughter, Saya's mother begins sending her recorded bedtime stories inspired by Haitian folktales. Impacted by her parents' stories and letters, Saya writes a letter of her own in an attempt to bring her mother home.

Diaz, A. (2015). *The only road*. New York, NY: Simon & Schuster. (Gr. 3–7)

After the death of his cousin and best friend in his small Guatemalan town ruled by a violent gang known for drug trafficking, Jaime fears he might be a future target and decides to flee with his cousin. Based on true events, *The Only Road* shares the story of twelve-year-old Jaime's perilous journey from Guatemala to the United States to live with his brother and find a chance at a better life.

Faruqi, R. (2015). *Lailah's lunchbox: A Ramadan story*. (Gr. K–3)
Lailah recently moved to Georgia from Abu Dhabi and is struggling to fit in. She is finally old enough to fast for Ramadan but is worried that her new classmates won't understand why she is skipping lunch. With guidance from her teacher and school librarian, Lailah discovers new friends who respect her beliefs and welcome her to their school.

Foreman, M. (2015). *The seeds of friendship*. Boston, MA: Candlewick. (PreK–2)
Adam is new to urban life in the United States and misses his African home. He fills his room with pictures of his friends and the elephants, hippos, lions, and landscapes he loves. In winter, he creates snow animals in his new neighborhood and makes new friends, but he still misses the green of his native country. When a teacher gives him some seeds, Adam is inspired to bring green into his concrete environment.

Grande, R. (2016). *The distance between us: Young readers edition*. New York, NY: Aladdin. (Gr. 6–9)
Reyna and her siblings are left to live with their grandmother after her parents decide to make their way illegally across the Mexican/U.S. border. After hardships, Reyna realizes that she must make the dangerous journey herself. In this middle-grade adaption of her memoir, Grande tells the story of her journey to "El Otro Lado" and her struggle as she tries to adjust to a new language, culture, and defined family.

Kobald, I. (2015). *My two blankets*. New York, NY: Houghton Mifflin Harcourt. (Gr. 1–4)
When Cartwheel moves to a new country with her aunt, everything is strange. Her old blanket comforts her and she begins to equate it to her past, and to her comfort with her native language. As she makes a new friend, learns a new language, and adjusts to her new life, she gets a new blanket. Now she has two blankets, two languages, and two homes.

Lorenzi, N. D. (2016). *A long pitch home*. New York, NY: Charlesbridge. (Gr. 4–7)
Ten-year-old Bilal moved to Virginia from Pakistan. He misses his old life and the sport of cricket, at which he was a star. Most of all, he misses his father, who had to stay behind. Bilal struggles to learn English, make friends, adjust to strange American customs, and learn the strange sport of baseball. He hopes that if he can become good at baseball then his father will be able to make it to the United States to watch him play.

> O'Brien, A. S. (2015). *I'm new here*. New York, NY: Charlesbridge. (Gr. K–2)
> Three new students join a classroom, and each struggles to fit in and learn a new language. Maria, from Guatemala, finds new friends playing soccer. Jin, from Korea, makes a new friend by teaching Korean words. And Fatimah, from Somalia, finds the courage to share her artwork and find other art lovers to spend time with. All three find acceptance from their classmates and begin to adjust to their new environment.
>
> Watts, J. (2016). *A piece of home*. Boston, MA: Candlewick. (Gr. K–2)
> Hee Jun's family moves to West Virginia from Korea, and he has a hard time adjusting to his new home. He looks and sounds different from his classmates, and he can't understand what his teacher is saying. His mouth just doesn't want to speak English. Slowly, Hee Jun makes new friends and learns English, but West Virginia doesn't feel like home until he sees a familiar flower from Korea in his new friend's garden.
>
> Weeks, S., & Varadarajan, G. (2016). *Save me a seat*. New York, NY: Scholastic. (Gr. 3–6)
> Ravi and Joe don't think they have anything in common except that they both are stuck in school. Ravi recently moved to the United States from India and is adjusting to his new life and language. Joe's best friends recently moved away and he's adjusting to life at school without them. When Joe and Ravi both become the targets of the school bully, they get to know one another as they work together to face a common enemy.

Literature as a Window to Multilingualism

Literature can also be utilized to celebrate learners' evolving multilingualism. This lens capitalizes on literature that includes elements of bi-, tri-, or plurilingualism within the pages the ELs are reading. It explores how culturally relevant picture books can validate the lives of all learners in today's classrooms.

The use of bilingual (or tri- or plurilingual) literature in the class is not common practice, and such books can be a challenge to find. But the search is worth it. To children who grow up in plurilingual environments, it is their norm to see people in their lives communicating using one or more languages within a single setting. Seeing their lives reflected in books shows students that this is a valuable commodity, and the valuing of the plurilingual sociocultural context is one of the most important determiners of academic success (Daniel, 2016; Garcia & Wei, 2014). Books that celebrate the unique strengths of multilingual individuals help ELs negotiate understandings across their worlds. When ELs read through a multilingual lens they become aware that their plurilingualism is something to be proud of, and that regardless of their language proficiency, their languages help them communicate and learn about others.

Translanguaging is "the ability of multilingual speakers to shuttle between languages, treating the diverse languages that form their repertoire as an integrated system" (Canagarajah, 2011, p. 401). Inclusive multilingual instruction requires that teachers acknowledge all of their students' languages and capitalize on them as vehicles to comprehension and language development. Culturally relevant literature provides the translanguaging spaces ELs need to become strategic readers.

Effective English language teaching involves understanding and encouraging the reality of learners' translanguaging (Garcia & Wei, 2014) and acknowledging that engaging narrative texts are beginning scaffolds to academic and life-long success. Teachers need to ensure that learners have opportunities to use discourse features from all their languages within a communicative framework (Nation, 2009). By critically examining the literature used in the classroom, teachers can give all students opportunities to use and celebrate their diverse language abilities while they are acquiring English.

In addition to books that incorporate multiple languages within their pages, there are books that highlight the experiences of ELs as they learn English. Ghiso and Campano (2013) identified four categories of books that depict issues of multilingualism, specifically, books that incorporate multilingualism at home, in school, in the neighborhood, and lastly the idea of silence as a means of identifying and determining a language identity. These books promote discussion of the different ways being multilingual plays into ELs' daily lives and provides space for them to critically reflect on the beliefs and values around language in greater society. Through this lens, plurilingualism can be conceptualized "as an epistemic opportunity to foster new understandings, views, and narratives" (Ghiso & Campano, 2013, p. 54).

Teachers promote biliteracy by consciously examining if the picture books they have selected for their classrooms give all students opportunities to use their diverse language abilities while they are acquiring English. Choose books that lend themselves to implementing multilingual pedagogies. Rhyming books can serve well to model writing, as many of these do not represent a single culture but will lend themselves to applications across cultures. In her work with ELs, this chapter's second author found that books that begin with the words "There was an old woman" were well received by ELs and lent themselves to the creation of new stories that the children could adapt to their world.

Harking back to when she (second author) was a pull-out English as a second language classroom teacher, she remembers an inquisitive and competitive triad of ELs from Japan, Mexico, and Peru. The students enjoyed playing with the English language they were learning so their teacher gave them the opportunity to link reading, writing, and drawing. Together the group wrote books with words that rhymed and included illustrations that took them back to homelands that reflected their familial cultures.

Ideas flowed from home to school and as the background of the stories emerged, each student learned about the cultural capital of their classmates. The ELs brought items from home to show their friends, and when the stories were finished, they read them to their monolingual classmates. The products included a book with an elegant old woman dressed in a beautiful kimono who slept on a mat, a man who painted wall murals from Oaxaca, Oaxaca, and a mother who herded her guinea pigs together for their nightly feeding.

Using Literature Strategically

In addition to using culturally relevant literature through a multicultural and a multilingual lens, it can also be used to teach strategies. Learning English cannot be reduced to formulas and techniques; it takes a personal knowledge of students' backgrounds and skills to make teaching effective. Culturally relevant literature can be an effective tool to teach ELs pre-, during-, and post-reading strategies. It provides an entry point into reading and vocabulary instruction by situating learning within ELs' individual worlds.

It is easier for ELs to comprehend and develop metacognitive skills when using books that mirror their communities. Books that capture students' interests provide a medium that eases the transition from reading for aesthetic purposes to reading strategically for efferent purposes.

Students acquire meaning of new words when they use them in context, especially when it comes to the learning of idioms and expressions.

Through the use of conversations focused on ways to extract meaning from text, ELs are given opportunities to use language as scaffolds to reach higher levels of understandings. Teachers have opportunities to design these scaffolds and to help create strategic readers able to question the perspectives of the people in their communities. Holding class discussions based on culturally relevant literature will expedite this process.

Effective scaffolds teach ELs how to identify strategies that empower them as they are working to understand the target language of study. Teaching ELs to use pre-reading strategies helps them examine, acknowledge, and respect the differences they see between their classmates and themselves. Effective during-reading strategies consider students' learning styles and provide translanguaging spaces that foster natural processes in second language acquisition at the same time students develop understandings about different cultures (Garcia & Wei, 2014). Post-reading strategies help students find their voice and develop a sense of citizenship. When ELs read literature that mirrors their cultures of origin, it is easier for them to use the strategies they are learning and increase their comprehension of text.

Raising Metacognitive Awareness: Reading Strategically

Daniel (2016) discusses the power that teachers have to guide their students and situate them on the path to academic success. She emphasizes the need for instruction that helps ELs develop their procedural and declarative knowledge. Daniel is concerned with ELs' access to the meaning of texts and their having the capability to explain the strategies they use to do so. She tells us:

> Students demonstrate their *declarative knowledge* when they access their schemata (prior knowledge) to explain their understandings (explain what they have mastered). Learners use *procedural knowledge* when they complete tasks efficiently (they have the requisite mastery to know what to do). (Daniel, 2016, p. 100)

ELs in U.S. schools represent many countries' schooling systems. This is not only because they may have lived in different geographical areas and attended school in different continents but also because their close relatives may have experienced only teacher-led instruction as the norm. When familial expectations lead to misunderstanding of schooling requirements, the children suffer if no one is present to help them navigate across their worlds.

In your classroom, engage learners in tasks that will ensure they become strategic readers able to read for aesthetic and efferent purposes. Teach them to become strategic interpreters of text and illustrations. Select instructional strategies that will turn the ELs into efficient readers who are aware of how they construct meaning. Much of what teachers do in mainstream classrooms will empower all learners to strategize. Make sure to teach ELs the following strategies and incorporate a focus on mastery of an additional language:

- Picture walks (before reading)
- Think, Pair, Share (during reading)
- T-charts that young learners can complete in dyads by drawing pictures (after reading)
- Venn diagrams that include word banks (before and after reading)
- Right there in-the-text questions (during the reading process)
- Compare and contrast activities (during and after reading)
- Beyond the text questions (during and after reading)
- K-W-L (throughout the entire reading process)

DESIGNING BRIGHTER FUTURES

Culturally relevant children's literature holds great possibilities for cultivating ELs' multicultural understandings, celebrating their diverse cultural backgrounds and identities, scaffolding their academic success in multiple languages, accepting and honoring their linguistic and cultural pluralism, and influencing their reading motivation and literacy growth (Ghiso & Campano, 2013; Martinez-Roldán, 2005; Wolf, 2004).

Children's books that portray authentic snapshots into other cultures that represent the current student demographic of our classrooms offer promises to tomorrow's world citizens. Using authentic books provides an opportunity for creating learning environments that validate ELs and their families' life experiences.

Recommendations for the Classroom

1. Teach students the value of reading strategically. Every minute of the school day, students are living in a world replete with print. Collaborate with your colleagues to identify ways to help learners see that pulling out the key ideas in everything they read equates to understanding the important ideas authors convey.

2. Teach students how to critically evaluate the books that they read. Similar to the suggestions we've listed above for you to consider when selecting literature for your classroom, go over some evaluative criteria with students, and have them analyze the literature for cultural accuracy, authenticity, and inclusion.

3. Allow students to take ownership of classroom discussions. Literature circles provide an excellent opportunity for students to become active in book discussions and make critical connections. Allow students to choose a book to read from a selection you provide. Then assign students roles (or allow them to self-select their roles) for them to take on during small-group discussion. Common literature circle roles include discussion director, connector, literary luminary, vocabulary enricher, character captain, and artistic adventurer.

4. Do not fear addressing difficult topics in the classroom. You may not know what challenges parents are facing and what topics they would like you to include in classroom conversations. You might prepare a survey to elicit parental input that will help you select books for the classroom.

Technology Resources

1. Teachers know that current technologies help students learn. They devote time to evaluate technology applications and how these might promote vocabulary development, add visuals that support comprehension for the ELs, and so on. Consider too that technology will you keep you abreast of new books that are appropriate for today's student demographic. The following

websites will help you select books written in different languages to expand the offerings in school and in your classroom library:

- Bab'l Books at http://bablbooks.com
- Children's Book Press at www.leeandlow.com/imprints/4
- Lectorum at www.lectorum.com
- Pan Asian Publications at www.panap.com
- Cinco Puntos Press at www.cincopuntos.com
- Asia for Kids at www.afk.com

2. Every year, explore books identified as outstanding examples of culturally responsive literature. Consult award lists and notable lists for titles of note.

- The American Library Association Youth Media Awards (www.ala.org/awardsgrants/awards/browse) and Children's Notables lists (www.ala.org/alsc/awardsgrants/notalists). These websites provide links to a multitude of annual awards and notables lists, many of which focus on identifying quality culturally relevant literature. Focus on the winners of the Batchelder and Pura Belpré awards.
- The International Literacy Association's Children's Literature/Reading Special Interest Group publishes an annual Notable Books for a Global Society list (http://clrsig.org/nbgs.php). Books that make this list enhance student understanding of people and cultures throughout the world.
- The Jane Addams Children's Book Awards (www.janeaddamspeace.org/jacba). This award is given annually to children's books that promote peace, social justice, world community, and the equality of all sexes and races

3. Explore the International Children's Digital Library: A Library for the World's Children (http://en.childrenslibrary.org/index.shtml). The ICDL Foundation provides free online access to a range of international children's literature with the goal of promoting tolerance and respect for diverse cultures, languages, and ideas.

4. Explore websites designed to provide culturally responsive classroom ideas that utilize culturally relevant literature.

- Inclusive Classrooms Project (http://inclusiveclassrooms.org/practice/culturally-relevant-curriculum)
- Colorín Colorado (www.colorincolorado.org/article/culturally-relevant-books-ell-classroom)
- Teaching Tolerance (www.tolerance.org/classroom-resources)

- Teacher Vision (www.teachervision.com/teacher-resources/printable/33631.html)

REFERENCES

Au, K. (2001). Culturally responsive instruction as a dimension of new literacies. *Reading Online, 5*(1), 1–11.

Bishop, R. S. (1990). Mirrors, windows, and sliding glass doors. *Perspectives: Choosing and Using Books for the Classroom, 6*(3), ix–xi.

Bishop, R. S. (1992). Multicultural literature for children: Making informed choices. In V. Harris (Ed.), *Teaching multicultural literature in grades K-8* (pp. 37–54). Norwood, MA: Christopher-Gordon.

Bourdieu, P. (1987). What makes a social class? On the theoretical and practical existence of groups. *Berkeley Journal of Sociology, 32*, 1–17.

Brown, H. D. (2007). *Principles of language learning and teaching* (5th ed.). White Plains, NY: Pearson and Longman.

Canagarajah, S. (2011). Codemeshing in academic writing: Identifying teachable strategies of translanguaging. *The Modern Language Journal, 95*(3), 401–417.

Ching, S. H. D. (2005). Multicultural children's literature as an instrument of power. *Language Arts, 83*(2), 128–136.

Colby, S. A., & Lyon, A. F. (2004). Heightening awareness about the importance of using multicultural literature. *Multicultural Education, 11*(3), 24–28.

Council for Interracial Books for Children. (1974). *10 quick ways to analyze children's books for racism and sexism*. Retrieved from http://alimichael.org/wp-content/uploads/2012/02/10ways-to-analyze-Children-books-for-racism.pdf

Cummins, J. (2003). Reading and the bilingual students: Fact and friction. In G. G. Garcia (Ed.), *English learners: Reaching the highest level of English literacy* (pp. 2–33). Newark, DE: International Reading Association.

Cummins, J. (2009). Pedagogies of choice: Challenging coercive relations of power in classrooms and communities. *International Journal of Bilingual Education and Bilingualism*, 2 (3), 261–271.

Daniel, M. (2016). Critical pedagogy's power in English language teaching. In L. R. Jacobs & C. Hastings (Eds.), *The importance of social justice in English language teaching* (pp. 25–38). Alexandria, VA: TESOL Press.

Daniel, M. (2016). Planning instruction for English language learners: Strategies teachers need to know. In D. Schwarzer & J. Grinberg (Eds.), *Successful teaching: What every novice teacher needs to know* (pp. 89–116). Lanham, MD: Rowman & Littlefield.

DeLeón, L. (2002). Multicultural literature: Reading to develop self-worth. *Multicultural Education*, 10 (2), 49–51.

Dixson, A. D., & Fasching-Varner, K. J. (2009). This is how we do it: Helping teachers understand culturally relevant pedagogy in diverse classrooms. In C. Compton-Lilly (Ed.), *Breaking the silence: Recognizing the social and cultural resources students bring to the classroom* (p. 34–48). Newark, DE: International Reading Association.

Gangi, J. M. (2008). The unbearable whiteness of literacy instruction: Realizing the implications of the proficient reader research. *Multicultural Review, 17*(1), 30–35.

Garcia, O., & Wei, L. (2014). *Translanguaging: Language, bilingualism, and education*. London, England: Palgrave MacMillan.

Gay, G. (2000). *Culturally responsive teaching: Theory, research, & practice*. New York, NY: Teachers College Press.

Gay, G. (2002). Preparing for culturally responsive teaching. *Journal of Teacher Education, 53*(2), 106–116.

Ghiso, M. P., & Campano, G. (2013). Ideologies of language and identity in U.S. children's literature. *Bookbird: A Journal of International Children's Literature, 51*(3), pp. 47–55.

González, N., Moll, L., & Amanti, C. (Eds.) (2005). *Funds of knowledge for teaching in Latino households*. Mahwah, NJ: Lawrence Erlbaum Associates.
Gray, E. S. (2009). The importance of visibility: Students' and teachers' criteria for selecting African American literature. *The Reading Teacher, 62*(6), 472–481.
Guthrie, J. T., McGough, K., Bennett, L., & Rice, M. E. (1996). Concept-oriented reading instruction to develop motivational and cognitive aspects of reading. In L. Baker, P. Afflerbach, & D. Reinking (Ed.), *Developing engaged readers in school and home communities* (pp. 165–190). Mahwah, NJ: Erlbaum
Guthrie, J. T., & Wigfield, A. (2000). Engagement and motivation in reading. In M. L. Kamil, P. B. Mosenthal, P. D. Pearson, & R. Barr (Eds.), *Handbook of reading research* (Vol. 3, pp. 403–422). Mahwah, NJ: Lawrence Erlbaum Associates.
Guthrie, J. T., Wigfield, A., Barbosa, P., Perencevich, K. C., Taboada, A., Davis, M. H., ... Tonks, S. (2004). Increasing reading comprehension and engagement through concept-oriented reading instruction. *Journal of Educational Psychology, 96*(3), 403–423.
Heflin, B. R., & Barksdale-Ladd, M. A. (2001). African American children's literature that helps students find themselves: Selection guidelines for grades K-3. *The Reading Teacher, 54*(8), 810–819.
Howard, T. C. (2003). Culturally relevant pedagogy: Ingredients for critical teacher reflection. *Theory into Practice, 42*(3), 195–202.
Hughes-Hassell, S., Barkley, H., & Koehler, E. (2009). Promoting equity in children's literacy instruction: Using a critical race theory framework to examine transitional books. *School Library Media Research, 12*, 1–20.
Kelley, M., Wilson, N. S., & Koss, M. D. (2012). Using young adult literature to motivate and engage the disengaged. In J. A. Hayn & J. S. Kaplan (Eds.), *Teaching young adult literature today: Insights, considerations and perspectives for the classroom teacher* (pp. 77–98). Lanham, MD: Rowman & Littlefield
Landt, S. M. (2011). Integration of multicultural literature in primary grade language arts curriculum. *Journal of Multiculturalism in Education, 7*, 1–27.
Larson, J. & Marsh, J. (2005). *Making literacy real: Theories and practices for learning and teaching*. Thousand Oaks, CA: Sage.
Lohfink, G. (2010). The nature of Mexican American third graders' engagement with culturally relevant picture books. *Bilingual Research Journal, 33*(3), 346–363.
Martinez, M., Koss, M. D., Johnson, N. J. (2016). Meeting characters in Caldecotts: What does this mean for today's readers? *The Reading Teacher, 70*(1), 19–28.
Martinez-Roldán, C. (2005). The inquiry acts of bilingual children in literature discussions. *Language Arts, 83*(1), 22–32.
McNair, J. C. (2010). Classic African American children's literature. *The Reading Teacher, 64*(2), 96–105.
Montgomery, W. (2001). Creating culturally responsive, inclusive classrooms. *Teaching Exceptional Children, 33*(4), 4–9.
Morrison, K. A., Robbins, H. H., & Rose, D. G. (2008). Operationalizing culturally relevant pedagogy: A synthesis of classroom based research. *Equity & Excellence in Education, 41*(4), 433–452.
Nation, I. S. P. (2009). *Teaching ESL/EFL reading and writing*. New York, NY: Routledge.
Peregoy, S. F., & Boyle, O. F. (2013). *Reading, writing, and learning in ESL: A resource book for teaching K-12 English learners* (6th ed.). Boston, MA: Pearson.
Rosenblatt, L. M. (1978). *The reader, the text, the poem: The transactional theory of the literary work*. Carbondale, IL: Southern Illinois University Press.
Ryan, A. M., & Patrick, H. (2001). The classroom social environment and changes in adolescents' motivation and engagement during middle school. *American Educational Research Journal, 38*(2), 437–460.
Souto-Manning, M. (2009). Negotiating culturally responsive pedagogy through multicultural children's literature: Towards critical democratic literacy practices in a first grade classroom. *Journal of Early Childhood Literacy, 9*(1), 50–74.

Taylor, B. M., Pearson, P. D., Peterson, D. S., & Rodriguez, M. C. (2003). Reading growth in high-poverty classrooms: The influence of teacher practices that encourage cognitive engagement in literacy learning. *The Elementary School Journal, 104*(1), 3–28.

TESOL/NCATE Teacher Standards Committee. (2009). *Standards for the recognition of initial TESOL programs in P-12 ESL teacher education (2010)*. Alexandria, VA: Teachers of English for Speakers of Other Languages. Retrieved from www.tesol.org

U.S. Census Bureau. (2013). Retrieved from www.census.gov/2013census/data

Wolf, S. (2004). *Interpreting literature with children*. Mahwah, NJ: Lawrence Erlbaum.

Yoon, B., Simpson, A., & Haag, C. (2010). Assimilation ideology: Critically examining underlying messages in multicultural literature. *Journal of Adolescent & Adult Literacy, 54*(2), 109–118.

II

Disciplinary Literacies

Chapter Three

Empowering ELs through Purposeful Writing Instruction in Content Areas

Guang-Lea Lee

Purposeful writing and learning in content area classrooms empowers English learners. The author's goal is to help teachers better understand how to incorporate purposeful and authentic writing experiences to teach grade-level content to ELs.

English learners (ELs) are empowered through collaborative and scaffolded learning of grade-level academic content and active participation in authentic literacy pedagogy. Through collaborative activities, teachers support ELs to ensure they gain proficiency in language and content learning tasks. Grounded on Vygotsky's (1978) socio-linguistic theory and concept of the zone of proximal development, Bruner (1983) claimed that children's language learning relies heavily on collaborative interactions and scaffolding provided by adults. Recently, several researchers (Kayi-Aydar, 2013; Peregoy & Boyle, 2013; Van Staden, 2011) who are influenced by Vygotsky and Bruner recommended that teachers use a variety of resources, support, and guidance for students learning new concepts beyond their current independent comprehension level.

Brassell and Furtado (2008) suggest that the best strategy teachers can use to enhance their students' literacy is to have them read and write frequently. This is challenging for ELs who are expected to read and write beyond their current reading level in English. Thus, teachers of ELs need to provide appropriate scaffolding for students to comprehend the academic language. Effective scaffolding uses cultural examples, small-group discussions, and purposeful writing to reduce language barriers and engage ELs in active participation through inquiry. Vygotsky's (1978) scaffolding theory helps teachers understand how to promote collaboration between ELs and their monolingual English-speaking peers and teachers.

Long ago, Cummins (1994) advised teachers to create a classroom environment for empowering ELs. Empowered ELs are not silent members of the classroom community. They are active participants who are aware that it is safe to inquire as to the lesson's meaning and focus. In keeping with his previous assertions, Cummins (2011) more recently claimed that low-income ELs who have actively interacted and engaged with literacy in a print-rich environment are more likely to close the achievement gap.

Teachers should support ELs and encourage them to ask critical questions, such as when, why, how, and who, to set a purpose for learning. ELs should collaborate and participate in conversations with their advanced peers (Mercer, Dawes, & Staarman, 2009) so that they will expand their knowledge and co-construct their own meaning of content based on their experiences in their two cultures. When engaged in collaboration with more competent English speakers, ELs are often able to grasp higher levels of content than their English proficiency level indicates.

Also, when teachers praise ELs' attempts to use language, and provide them with modeling and scaffolding, they can gain content knowledge while acquiring English language skills. Teachers need to understand that ELs may have already acquired oral language and constructed concepts in their home language; thus, the use of visuals and realia (artifacts) from real life is beneficial to their learning of new content vocabulary as it connects with their own cultures and experiences.

With teacher scaffolding and in collaboration with peers, ELs are capable of adding new English sounds and meanings to the existing context of their home language. By the time many ELs begin their formal schooling in the United States they have already developed concepts in their heritage languages, and possess nontraditional funds of knowledge from their home and community (González, 2005). Prior knowledge gained in their first language supports their connections to new input. Being able to talk and write about their prior experiences, personal identities, and heritage culture (Cummins & Early, 2010) offers ELs opportunities to use language more meaningfully.

Krashen's (2013) Comprehensible Input Hypothesis directs teachers to make sure the lessons they present are meaningful, accessible, and understandable to each EL (Lucas, Villegas, & Freedson-Gonzalez, 2008; Rodrigo, Krashen, & Gribbons, 2004). An important condition for second language acquisition to occur is to keep in mind that the learners are able to comprehend input language that contains structure a bit beyond their current level of competence. This facilitative level of input is ensured through providing supportive instruction to ELs so that they can achieve at higher levels (Hammond, 2008; Read, 2010).

Effective teachers create educational settings and carefully select the classroom tasks required of ELs, so they can interact and learn alongside their more fluent English-speaking peers, not only in the classroom but also during nonacademic moments such as lunch and recess. Culturally proficient educators provide ELs frequent opportunities to write about prior experiences gained in the native language, and what they are currently learning, so they can internalize and demonstrate their knowledge in the specific content area they are studying (Hadaway & Young, 2006; Williams & Pilonieta, 2012).

PURPOSEFUL WRITING

Purposeful writing is designed to give ELs an opportunity to express a personal meaning for each learning activity and includes several distinctive characteristics. It is meaningful, relevant, and useful to students; focuses on the writing process over the product; supports students with a print-rich environment; provides choice within a variety of forms and genres; allows an experience of the recursive writing process; and gives an opportunity to interact with peers and teachers in response to text.

Some researchers (Assaf & Johnson, 2014; Samway, 2006) emphasize that purposeful writing motivates students to learn across the content to solve real issues that matter and promote a better society. Although purposeful, real-world writing takes time and effort, it is a useful process to help students generate a piece of authentic writing ranging from letters, stories, reports, persuasive explanations, movie scripts, and quick writes, to reflective essays.

In purposeful writing students are able to convey meaning to an audience. This stimulates their curiosity about new content and engages them in creative literary work (Young & Rasinski, 2013). Writing is an essential learning tool, as it helps students think and construct new concepts and learn through active participation in interpersonal interactions and interpretive processes. Meaningful writing activities that require ELs to trace back to prior experiences, familiar concepts, and their home culture best promote second language acquisition and learning.

Learning activities using purposeful writing are only meaningful, however, to the extent that they create a connection between school and life experiences. Purposeful writing is useful to empower ELs to the extent it allows them to present their personal stories and culture. When content-area lessons reflect their culture and community, they become meaningful, and ELs are more motivated to learn.

Teachers who use the suggested instructional activities included in this chapter will need to recognize the unique ethnicity of all students, embrace their cultural and ethnic traditions, involve parents, and incorporate the ELs' home life in their instruction. When their unique personal experiences, culture, and language are accepted in their learning, social justice is achieved for the ELs who come to know that their opinions are valued (Daniel, 2016). Many researchers encourage teachers to use students' home language in the classroom, even when they themselves are monolingual. This may be necessary to clarify directions, or provide explicit instruction to the EL whose English language proficiency inhibits full comprehension (Cary, 2007).

Even though ELs' written English may contain grammatical and semantic errors and not follow rules of proper conventional English, teachers can respond to the intended meanings being communicated. Krashen (2013) emphasized that ELs need to use language as much as possible in order to achieve communicative fluency. Otherwise, they may feel overwhelmed and pay too much attention to the form of the language, rather than the meaning they are conveying through speaking and writing. When teachers encourage ELs to take risks and accept and view their mistakes as part and parcel of the process, the students will feel more comfortable and be more motivated to attempt to speak their new language with purpose.

Watts-Taffe and Truscott (2000) suggested that increasing the degree to which learning situations are context-rich is a way of scaffolding the development of both social and Cognitive Academic Language Proficiency (CALP) among ELs. According to Cummins (2000), although many ELs achieve proficiency in basic interpersonal communication skills (BICS)—context-rich language used during activities, such as playing or cooking, for example—they tend to experience difficulty with academic language acquisition.

Unlike social language learning, it takes an average of five to seven years for ELs to become proficient in academic language use (Cummins, 1994; Hakuta, Butler, & Witt, 2000). Thus, while ELs are becoming proficient in academic English, teachers need to incorporate personal experience during instructional time that offers context-reduced academic terminology (Dimino, Taylor, & Morris, 2015). Gutiérrez-Clellen, Simon-Cereijido, and Sweet (2012) reported that a significant predictor of English language proficiency is the level of the child's first language skills.

APPLICATIONS OF PURPOSEFUL WRITING IN MRS. JOHNSON'S CLASSROOM

While keeping in mind the theories and available research in language and literacy acquisition for ELs, teachers can apply purposeful and engaging writing experiences to enhance vocabulary and content knowledge, as well as basic communication skills. To illustrate the application of purposeful writing in a classroom, an example of a teacher who created opportunities in a mainstream classroom for students to write with purpose will now be presented. This section uses pseudonyms for the teacher (Mrs. Susan Johnson: Mrs. J.) and EL student (Pedro Martinez). After introducing Pedro's story, the author chronicles the approaches Mrs. J. took to support Pedro's improvement in language and academic learning.

Mrs. J. had been teaching for ten years and had a master's degree in elementary education. She had taught ELs in the past and enjoyed working with diverse students and families. She was teaching a social studies unit on "Honoring Our Nation's Heroes" to her third-grade students in an inclusion classroom at an urban school in eastern Virginia. The lesson introduced here focuses on identifying the contributions of Martin Luther King Jr. and César Chavez. Comparing and contrasting ideas and perspectives to better understand people and events in world culture is a standard of learning (SOL) for third-grade history and social science (Virginia Board of Education, 2008). One way teachers can address the standards is to have students write short reports that include descriptive details that elaborate on the central idea.

Pedro Martinez was eight years old when he enrolled in Mrs. J.'s third-grade class for the 2015–2016 school year. According to his school records from El Salvador, he had attended school regularly beginning at age five and had attained grade-level literacy skills in Spanish. Pedro was fluent in speaking, able to read complex sentences, and had a large vocabulary in Spanish. He was especially advanced in his ability to add, subtract, and multiply, and one of his primary interests was learning math. His thinking ability and desire for learning were there, but he could not fully understand and process English texts in the content areas.

Soon after Pedro's father moved to the United States from El Salvador as a migrant worker, he petitioned for his eight-year-old son to join him. Pedro was excited to move to the United States to live with his father, aunt, and several cousins—all in the same house. He was heartbroken, though, because his mother and older sisters remained in El Salvador. For some reason unknown to his teacher, they could not move with Pedro. Mrs. J. did not know too much about the family's background other than that Pedro's father spoke very little English and worked many hours to support his family. Pedro spoke Spanish at home and was a shy, quiet student at school, but very attentive to the teacher, and well behaved.

When Pedro first arrived in Mrs. J.'s class, he was very frustrated. He could not speak English nor understand what his teacher and classmates were saying. Soon after school began, Pedro's reading started to improve but his writing skills developed much more slowly, and he did not like to elaborate or expand on his written responses. When faced with a writing assignment, he would often copy directly from a book or copy the teacher's modeled writing on the whiteboard. At first the teacher allowed Pedro to write only a few words in English, or on a topic of his choosing, including family stories in Spanish.

After nine months, he had gained essential oral language skills and was rapidly improving in pronunciation, sight words, spelling, word analysis, vocabulary, and content knowledge. He still spoke with a heavy accent but could understand what he read in English. Although his oral and written communication were at a minimum, his listening comprehension was sufficient to follow the teacher's directions, practice the vocabulary the class was learning, and participate in purposeful writing activities to learn in the content areas.

INFORMAL CONVERSATIONS

Mrs. J. set aside at least fifteen minutes to have a daily conversation with Pedro about what they would be working on in class that day. She believed that conversations are valuable learning processes that stimulate thinking and support the construction of new concepts. She initiated a brief dialog to determine Pedro's prior knowledge and introduce new concepts, such as the terms "I have a dream" speech and "migrant worker." She found that when Pedro did not understand a question, his response tended to be "yes." This is illustrated in the vignette below.

Mrs. J.: Do you want to have a morning talk with me?

Pedro: Yes.

Mrs. J.: When did you move from El Salvador?

Pedro: Yes.

Mrs. J.: I know you came from El Salvador in September. So, you say, I came from El Salvador in September.

Pedro: Yes, I came from El Salvador in September.

Mrs. J.: What do you think *migrant* means?

Pedro: (Responded by only shaking head)

Mrs. J.: You came to the United States last year with your father. You and your father are a migrant family.

Pedro: Yes (responded as nodding). Birds move too.

Mrs. J.: That's correct. Birds are migrant as well to find food and a better place. How long you have been here? Let's count, September, October, November . . . and May.

Pedro: I don't know [how to say it in English.]. I know Spanish.

Mrs. J.: Let's use our app! (She opened a laptop translation app and showed him how to use it.)

Pedro: Ah ha! (He smiled big and practiced learning the new words.)

Mrs. J.: I have another question. Why did your father move to America?

Pedro: My dad want job. He have job.

Mrs. J.: Yes, it is wonderful that he has a good job. He decided to move to the United States to find a job. What was his dream for life in America? Dream means a very strong wish.

Pedro: Because he job here.

Mrs. J.: Yes, he found a job here so he could achieve his wish.

After the dialog, Pedro drew and wrote about his father's job as a migrant worker—which was related to the lesson on César Chavez. ELs such as Pedro who have not acquired writing proficiency should be allowed to write in their first language when appropriate scaffolding for simple sentence writing cannot be provided. ELs can use a translation application (app) and write using their laptop computer, typing in a Word document instead of writing by hand. This can assist them in recognizing and correcting misspelled words as they type. Pedro was very eager to participate in dialogs with his teacher and peers to learn English, and he loved working with them. He quickly became discouraged, though, as he found it difficult to fully express his needs in the classroom.

As seen in the above vignette, Mrs. J. encouraged Pedro to use the class laptop to translate and communicate his needs and thoughts. She also provided directions to assignments in Spanish using the translation app. She would speak into the translation app in English, and it would print the words on the screen in Spanish. Pedro and his teacher made good use of this tool, beginning with simple words or conversational phrases to communicate. It helped Pedro gain confidence in speaking and working in the classroom.

As shown from the above conversation with Pedro, although his syntax is incorrect, he had developed more than just survival words. After nine months of struggling to make sense of the sounds and rhythms of English, he gained knowledge of the pragmatic cues of language, and could put useful phrases together to make sentences. Mrs. J. initiated informal conversations before introducing any new concepts and assigned an English-speaking peer to help and interact with Pedro. His interaction with the teacher and peers helped him acquire English sound patterns, sentence formats, communication skills, and vocabulary.

Mrs. J. frequently communicated with the ESL tutor to make sure she covered basic phrases and prepositions useful in comprehending the subjects Pedro studied. Her collaboration with the ESL tutor was extremely important because Pedro needed to spend extra time to learn basic sight words and the Fry (2004) phrases such as *"in his ear, as for myself, yes it is, one by one, sit on the,* and so on."

FRONTLOADING ACTIVITIES

Frontloading activities are useful to set the purpose for learning, introduce new information, and provide comprehensible input. Such activities include discussing academic vocabulary, singing a song to build vocabulary, watching a video clip, touching real things, viewing a picture chart of keywords, and defining vocabulary in students' own words (Echevarria, Vogt, & Short, 2004; Paquette & Rieg, 2008). The following section introduces frontloading activities that Mrs. J. used before her students read the grade-level social studies text focused on "Honoring Our Nation's Heroes." The objective of the lesson was to compare and contrast the lives and accomplishments of Dr. Martin Luther King Jr. and César Chavez.

Mrs. J. reviewed discipline-specific words through comparison and contrast, using objects found in the classroom—a desktop computer and a laptop computer. She asked, "What do these computers have in common, and what are their differences?" Mrs. J. also reviewed easier words, and the group would decide if these were different or the same. The class activity was to compare and contrast any two family members, for example, mother and sister, and write a few words about them and how they contribute to the family. To make sure your ELs understand the meaning of *compare* and *contrast*, attention can be drawn to Spanish cognates that they already know: *comparar* for compare and *contraste* for contrast.

The teacher prepared a word bank about the accomplishments of the two heroes, Dr. Martin Luther King Jr. and César Chavez. She then had students match labels to images from the Internet to introduce key concepts and new language: migrant, wages, consume, Nobel Peace Prize, segregation, equality, voting rights, race, strike, boycott, pickets, protest, freedom, and human rights. To build additional language proficiency, Mrs. J. engaged students in reading key phrases. These were posted on the classroom wall to be referenced during writing. Some examples were *sat in the yard, seemed very quiet, quite surprisingly, a year later, believe in, for many days, traveling around, awarded to honor, public speaking skills, believed that, instead of,* and *have the same rights as others.* Seeing words written on the board helps ELs to listen and comprehend. ELs can use them to review the meaning before reading the text.

Another useful frontloading activity is to show students pictures of the heroes and ask them to share what they know about them. Teachers need to acknowledge and make a list of student responses. They can mention local reference points, such as streets, schools, or buildings named after the heroes. After accepting various responses from several students, teachers can play interesting video clips about the subjects. While watching the videos, students write down key facts and compare the two heroes on a chart. Following this, pairs of students compare their summaries.

LOW-STAKES WRITING ACTIVITIES

Getting ELs to willingly participate in content-area writing can be especially challenging, as they need to not only apply their new content vocabulary but also build on their recently acquired English vocabulary as well. A large percentage of ELs have not yet acquired basic sight words in English. Providing ELs with low-stakes writing opportunities (also known as writing to learn and quick writes) will support them in learning sight words as well as content vocabulary.

With quick writes, writing done without concern for mechanics and rules, teachers can encourage ELs to take more risks, and gain access to multiple writing samples in a short time as they monitor students' ability to express their ideas in writing. Low-stakes writing is typically not graded, can be differentiated to meet the individual's needs, and is completed in a short amount of time. Students can describe personal thoughts about a new topic in their multimodal writing, which summarizes concepts learned. It can include texts, poetry, visuals, audio, video, or free writings about a given topic.

Mrs. J. used a Venn diagram (shown in figure 3.1) where students compared and contrasted the lives and contributions of Dr. Martin Luther King Jr. and César Chavez, using words and phrases found while reading the text. Once each student was finished comparing and contrasting the two heroes on the Venn diagram, the class created a group Venn diagram summarizing the information each child had already gathered. This whole-class activity strengthened student understanding of the lesson, and the class Venn diagram served as an anchor chart that would support independent writing at a later date.

Another low-stakes writing activity a teacher can implement is to read text together with ELs using a large book or text projected on a whiteboard and make a list of questions the students want to answer. For example, students can ask: Who is Dr. Martin Luther King Jr? How are people segregated? What was his job? Why did Dr. King decide to work for human rights? How did César Chávez come to the United States? Why did he strike? What are unfair wages? How did César Chávez become a leader? The teacher should be careful not to give away answers, but, instead, give sufficient time for students to write their answers. ELs need extra time to understand the questions, think about new information, and formulate a response. ELs need to have a chance to talk about what they read.

When students establish personal reasons for writing, rather than writing for the teacher to grade, they can make a connection between their lives and the content they are learning. Giving learners a chance to ask questions helps them recognize their own level of metacognition so that they can judge how much they already know about the content, and evaluate their level of interest in learning more. After making a list of questions, students should be given time to write their own answers after reading the text individually or in groups.

WRITING IN COLLABORATION WITH PEERS

Collaborative and interactive writing experiences engage and motivate students in a classroom to participate in writing practice (Williams & Pilonieta,

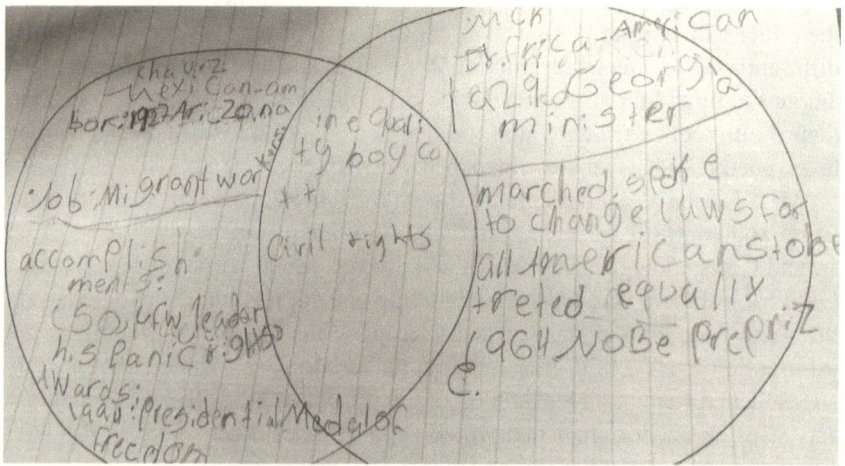

Figure 3.1. Pedro's Venn Diagram

2012). At the beginning of the school year, teachers need to create partner, small-group, and whole-class activities where students share stories, both orally and in writing, such as where they are from and what their favorite topics are in and out of school (Castro, 2015). Once a collaborative atmosphere is established, ELs will feel more comfortable participating in writing activities.

Mrs. J. divided the class into groups and had each group write important facts about their hero using complete sentences. The ELs initially worked in a small group to share and talk about the topic and outline, then joined in writing with more fluent writers. ELs often lack the confidence to take risks in their writing and, thus, expressing their thoughts orally before composing is of benefit to them.

To ensure equitable opportunities for speaking, listening, and writing activities for ELs, teachers can incorporate peer collaboration activities within heterogeneous groups. ELs need to receive clear directions and specific tasks, which can be written on the board. Mrs. J. assigned each group to write a draft history report on both important leaders listing five important facts with specific dates. She wrote the following list: Make small groups of four students; each child in the group will take turns speaking; select the best fact and write until you have five facts; each student must use a different color marker to write.

To ensure that there is not one dominant child who writes everything for the group, the teacher can make sure each student's color marker is used in their sentences. There should be five different color words or phrases in a sentence written by a group of five students. For example, "Dr. King led a boycott against riding buses holding a picket sign." Each group was invited to the front of class to show and read their written report. This is a great opportunity to teach language by explaining vocabulary, sentence structure, grammar, usage, conventions of spelling, and punctuation. The teacher can point out the key features of language rules students followed, such as irregular verbs, tense, and prepositional phrases.

If an EL has an idea, but cannot remember the English word, the student can write it in his or her home language. If no one can think of the corresponding English word, the teacher can use a translation app, and then write the English word next to the Spanish in parenthesis. This helps create strong connections with the new vocabulary, and also builds the EL's confidence as they share (Williams & Pilonieta, 2012).

JOINT WRITING WITH THE TEACHER

During joint writing, teachers demonstrate clear expectations for the topic, purpose, structure, and audience of the selected genre of student writing.

What is important is for students to pay attention to the overall structure of the writing which begins with a general statement, followed by the purpose and supporting details. An alternative way of modeling is allowing students in groups to analyze model essays of the same topic and identify the topic, purpose, and audience on their own. Teachers need to make sure that ELs can use the model writing as a sample and do not simply copy it word for word.

In the following example, the teacher shows how to write a report about the common contributions and accomplishments of Dr. Martin Luther King Jr. and César Chavez. During joint writing, she encourages students to identify the topic, purpose, and audience before they compose model sentences together. Mrs. J. begins modeling by writing on a SMART Board in front of the class while "thinking out loud."

> Well, what do I want to write about? I want to write about accomplishments of my heroes. . . . Who will need to read my writing? Well, my audience is my family. . . . Hmm, the purpose of my writing is to compare and contrast the accomplishments of the two heroes. I want to write my big idea I learned today about the two heroes and then add some detailed facts. Finally, I will identify the common beliefs and actions my heroes wanted me to follow.

From this point on, her students suggested ideas and continued their contributions and ideas to compose the following text (Mrs. J. writes with her students).

> Dr. King was a very good leader. He was born in 1929 in Georgia, and became an African American minister. He was a civil rights leader in the 1960s. He gave an "I Have a Dream" speech. He protested against segregated buses. He won the Nobel Peace Prize in 1964. Dr. King died from trying to be fair for black people. Without him, I would not be with all my friends.
>   Cesar Chavez was a great civil rights leader as well. Chavez was born in 1927 in Arizona. When he was young, he was a migrant farm worker. He became a leader for farm workers and made sure of better lives for them. He led boycotts for the people not to consume grapes or lettuce. People refused to purchase produce because they were on strike. He used nonviolent ways to demonstrate against wage discrimination. He informed people about their poor working conditions.
>   The two heroes spoke about equality. They fought for justice so all people would have equal rights. I respect both of my heroes and want to be like them.

Throughout the joint construction process, "the teacher and students constantly reread together what they have written, with the teacher asking questions like: Is that the best way to say it? Can anyone think of a more appropriate word than that?" (Gibbons, 2015, p. 177). This process allows teachers to discuss a better way to write, modeling how to revise a draft sentence. It is a chance to show students that good writing takes several corrections. For instance, when students want to write, "People didn't buy grapes, and they had a picket," the teacher can prompt them to reformulate it using academic vocabulary and write, "People refused to purchase produce because they were on strike."

INDEPENDENT WRITING

Independent writing encourages students to think and compose their own ideas to meet lesson objectives. Independent writing is an appropriate instructional task after students have developed sufficient background knowledge about the content and established a concrete purpose and audience for writing. Like all students, ELs need frequent opportunities to write about what they have learned. Meaningful contexts help students internalize and demonstrate their knowledge (Williams & Pilonieta, 2012).

For independent writing, students can explore different genres, and the teacher can give a variety of topics for them to choose from. Various genres for authentic purposeful writing can include: a biography, a persuasive essay explaining a personal belief, their own "I Have a Dream" speech, instructions on how to become a community leader, letter-writing to a great leader, invitation card to a favorite hero for a class party, multimedia reports, my hero in my family, my neighborhood leader, descriptions of a new award for a hero, radio announcement about the awards their heroes received, newspaper report on a historic event, or creating a picket sign for a current justice issue. Giving such writing choices creates a supportive classroom environment that allows all students to feel more comfortable when trying to use new vocabulary, phrases, and expressions when writing independently.

Until ELs are ready to write independently, they can do so paired with either a fluent writing classmate or the teacher. For example, ELs can participate in creating a visual timeline of the major events that occurred in Dr. King's and Mr. Chavez's lives for the historical content area lesson. Another example of scaffolding is using the writing frame shown below. Teachers can help ELs to write a central idea, identify related ideas, and include descriptive details that elaborate on the central idea. When a teacher introduces a writing frame in a supportive and encouraging way, the ELs will have a successful independent writing experience

Dr. King was born _____.
His job was _____.
He is famous for _____.
I want to be like _____ because he _____.
I respect _____ because he _____.

Pedro chose to write a mini-biography (figure 3.2) that included historical facts and the accomplishments of the two heroes he learned about.

RECOMMENDATIONS FOR ACTION AND RELEVANT RESOURCES

In this section practical recommendations are provided for teachers who work with ELs to encourage the students to develop their English language proficiency and engage in purposeful writing in content-area classes.

1. Encourage interactions with fluent English-speaking students. It is critical to understand that a second language is most effectively acquired through conversation and completion of collaborative activities. Monolingual students will learn from their peer ELs how people of other cultures are different, and similar, to themselves.

2. Create safe language-learning environments. Remember the concept of the affective filter, which refers to students' feelings, motives, needs, attitudes, and emotional states such as self-confidence and self-motivation. ELs who experience stress, anxiety, or discomfort in the classroom may filter out the information presented in class, making it unavailable for understanding. Provide ELs with academic and emotional support along with positive reinforcement.

3. Teach content-area vocabulary and phrases. Spend sufficient time during prewriting activities to help the ELs become familiar with your lesson's vocabulary, phrases, and grammatical structures. Create a list of keywords from the text before having ELs read it. Ask all students to write the content words in their notebooks. This will also help ELs build their own list of new words, and give them a sense of autonomy as learners. Language should be taught using visuals, synonyms, and antonyms, involving ELs in speaking and writing those words in full sentences to reinforce the meaning in context.

4. Use multimodal instruction. Content-area textbooks require the mastery of academic vocabulary and comprehension of context-reduced texts. Incorporate context-embedded and action-oriented activities, and provide scaffolds for academic words using games, charades, acting, visuals (pictures, movies), and other realia to enhance context and lower the difficulty of the content. Visual tools help students understand abstract concepts, sequence information with greater ease, and connect and develop personal and meaningful ideas. Invite the ELs to write about new concepts in the language of their choice, and allow them to add their own drawings and color them. Songs are great tools because important words and key phrases appear repeatedly. They help students remember names, homophones, and words that rhyme, which are especially difficult for ELs. Through repeatedly singing

Figure 3.2. Pedro's Independent Writing

and reciting simple lines, the ELs will eventually learn to recognize phonologically similar words based on the context in which they were used.

5. Accept writing errors and use these to monitor students' progress. While the ELs make progress in writing, focus on the comprehensibility of the overall message in ELs' written work. Making errors in written expressions is natural and shows that the EL is making progress. Silencing ELs by correcting too many nonstandard utterances and expressions is detrimental to their progress. As an example, one EL wrote, "He work hardly and she is mom." Instead of making multiple errors in red, the teacher can appreciate the EL for introducing the mother and encourage the effort of writing in a complete sentence. The teacher can decipher the student's intended meaning, and say it back to him with correct structure, "She works hard, and she is my mom." The teacher can take this opportunity to teach subject-verb agreement, and address appropriate pronouns. Take care to correct gently. For example, point out no more than one essential error that hurts overall meaning per day. A positive way to do this would be to say, "Excuse me, I want to be sure that I understand better what you just wrote. Can you explain this a little more for me?" This way, the teacher verifies the EL's intended meaning through friendly dialogue, instead of saying in a negative tone, "What?" or "I don't know what you mean."

RELEVANT RESOURCES

Technology plays an increasingly important role in today's school classrooms. The free apps listed below will fit well with your instructional planning in classrooms with ELs. Consult the following websites:

- The Pilot. A translation device called the Pilot comes with two earpieces that resemble small hearing aids and a smartphone application. Teacher and student both wear a small earpiece and converse with a smartphone between them. The device listens to the conversation and translates through the earpieces in real time, allowing for quite close-to-normal conversations. www.waverlylabs.com
- Spanish Cognates is a website that offers a list of Spanish-to-English cognates organized alphabetically, by classroom subject, and by the ending rule of the cognates (singular, plural, feminine, or masculine). Teachers who are working with Spanish-speaking students can incorporate cognates when teaching English in the classroom. http://spanishcognates.org
- Piktochart provides visual representations that limit the amount of text students must process. ELs can use the infographic creator with a variety of templates to comprehend new concepts found in content area text. http://www.piktochart.com

- FluentU is a website with real-world English videos from sources ranging from the television *Friends* episodes and the *Hunger Games* trailers, to documentaries, broadcast news, and interviews. ELs can be exposed to rich and diverse language context while enjoying videos and listening to conversations. www.fluentu.com/english
- Songs for Teaching is a site that provides recordings of music for teachers using songs to help students remember and promote content-area knowledge. www.songsforteaching.com
- Edmodo helps teachers assign classroom work as well as homework with their whole class or small groups. It is a medium for involving parents, who give permission for their child to open an account while they maintain access and are able to monitor all tasks. Teachers post questions about topics being studied and upload information for the students to use in collaborative activities. Edmodo is an easy and safe format for ELs to respond to the teacher and their classmates and gives teachers a quick snapshot into the learners' progress. http://www.edmodo.com
- ESL Kids is a resource available for purchase for teaching English as a second language students that includes flashcards, worksheets, classroom games, and children's song lyrics. http://www.esl-kids.com
- Google Translate can be used to provide instant translations of English words, phrases, and sentences to over a hundred languages. It allows students to express their ideas in their home language and/or to translate their thoughts to English. It exposes ELs to English vocabulary and sentence structure when their work is translated. Teachers can use Google Translate to gain access to their students' ideas when they write these in their home language. http://translate.google.com
- Duolingo will help teachers to know how to say a few words and phrases in a student's native language. This knowledge can be important in building a relationship with ELs. http://www.duolingo.com
- The Essay Map is a website that provides an interactive graphic organizer. Essay Map enables grades three to twelve students to organize, outline, and summarize their ideas. It helps ELs develop an outline that includes an introduction, main ideas, supporting details, and a conclusion. The finished map can be saved, e-mailed, and printed. www.readwritethink.org/files/resources/interactives/essaymap

CONCLUSION

Although learning and communicating in the content areas, both orally and in writing, is difficult for ELs, it is important that teachers believe in them as capable thinkers and competent speakers and writers. Teachers can highlight ELs' abilities during writing lessons and promote and build on their strengths. Writing lessons can be designed with ELs in mind so that they can engage in learning and experience success in writing. In your classrooms, value ELs' writing efforts, create multiple opportunities for them to write for a variety of purposes, and value the diverse perspectives and rich cultural experiences that ELs bring to the classroom.

Using purposeful writing applications in content-area classrooms, teachers can provide equitable opportunities for ELs to use their home language to support their new language acquisition, enhance their literacy skills, and reach their full academic potential. During purposeful writing applications, teachers should use participatory approaches, with students taking a lead role. Encourage ELs to listen, talk, and write during peer interactions and collaborative writing activities to facilitate metacognition and the learning of new content. When you incorporate writing for real audiences that is purposeful in all content-area classrooms, you will lead the ELs to master their new language, and ensure they enjoy learning in content-area classrooms.

REFERENCES

Assaf, L. C., & Johnson, J. (2014). A call for action: Engaging in purposeful, real-world writing. *Voices from the Middle, 21*(3), 24–33.
Brassell, D., & Furtado, L. (2008). Enhancing English as a second language students' vocabulary knowledge. *Reading Matrix: An International Online Journal, 8*(1), 111–116.
Bruner, J. (1983). *Child's talk: Learning to use language.* Oxford: Oxford University Press.
Cary, S. (2007). *Working with English language learners: Answers to teachers' top ten questions* (2nd ed.). Portsmouth, NH: Heinemann.
Castro, G. (2015). Helping English language learners succeed in school. *Education Digest, 80*(7), 44–47.
Cummins, J. (1994). The acquisition of English as a second language. In K. Spangenberg-Urbschat & R. Pritchard (Eds.), *Kids come in all languages: Reading instruction for ESL students.* Newark, DE: International Reading Association.
Cummins, J. (2000) *Language, power and pedagogy: Bilingual children in the crossfire.* Clevedon, UK: Multilingual Matters.
Cummins, J. (2011). Literacy engagement. *The Reading Teacher, 65*(2), 142–146.
Cummins, J., & Early, M. (2010). *Identity texts: The collaborative creation of power in multilingual schools.* Staffordshire, UK: Trentham Books Ltd.
Daniel, M. (2016). Critical pedagogy's power in English language teaching. In L. R. Jacobs & C. Hastings (Eds.), *The importance of social justice in English language teaching* (pp. 25–38). Alexandria, VA: TESOL Press.
Dimino, J. A., Taylor, M., & Morris, J. (2015). *Professional learning communities facilitator's guide for the What Works Clearinghouse practice guide: Teaching academic content and literacy to English learners in elementary and middle school* (REL 2015–105). Washington, DC: U.S. Department of Education.
Echevarria, J., Vogt, M., & Short, D. (2004). *Making content comprehensible for English language learners: The SIOP Model.* Boston, MA: Allyn and Bacon.
Fry, E. B. (2004). *Dr. Fry's 1000 instant words: The most common words for teaching reading, writing and spelling.* Garden Grove, CA: Teacher Created Resources.
Gibbons, P. (2015). *Scaffolding language scaffolding learning: Teaching second language learners in the mainstream classroom.* Portsmouth, NH: Heinemann.

González, N. (2005). Beyond culture: The hybridity of funds of knowledge. In N. González, L. Moll, & C. Amanti (Eds.), *Funds of knowledge: Theorizing practices in households, communities, and classrooms* (pp. 29–46). Mahwah, NJ: Lawrence Erlbaum.

Gutiérrez-Clellen, V., Simon-Cereijido, G., & Sweet, M. (2012). Predictors of second language acquisition in Latino children with specific language impairment. *American Journal of Speech-Language Pathology, 21*(1), 64–77.

Hadaway, N. L., & Young, T. A., (2006). Negotiating meaning through writing. In T. A. Young & N. L. Hadaway (Eds.), *Supporting the literacy development of English learners: Increasing success in all classrooms* (pp. 150–167). Newark, DE: International Reading Association.

Hakuta, K., Butler, Y. G., & Witt, D. (2000). *How long does it take English learners to attain proficiency?* Santa Barbara, CA: University of California Linguistic Minority Research Institute.

Hammond, J. (2008). Intellectual challenge and ESL students: Implications of quality teaching initiatives. *Australian Journal of Language and Literacy, 31*(2), 128.

Kayi-Aydar, H. (2013). Scaffolding language learning in an academic ESL classroom. *ELT Journal, 67*(3), 324–335.

Krashen, S. (2013). *Second language acquisition: Theory, applications, and some conjectures.* Cambridge, UK: Cambridge University Press.

Lucas, T., Villegas, A. M., & Freedson-Gonzalez, M. (2008). Linguistically responsive teacher education preparing classroom teachers to teach English language learners. *Journal of Teacher Education, 59*(4), 361–373.

Mercer, N., Dawes, L., & Staarman, J. K. (2009). Dialogic teaching in the primary science classroom. *Language and Education, 23*(4), 353–369.

Paquette, K. R., & Rieg, S. A. (2008). Using music to support the literacy development of young English language learners. *Early Childhood Education Journal, 36*(3), 227–232.

Peregoy, S. F., & Boyle, O. F. (2013). *Reading, writing, and learning in ESL: A resource book for teaching K-12 English learners* (6th ed.). Boston, MA: Pearson.

Read, S. (2010). A model for scaffolding writing instruction: IMSCI. *The Reading Teacher, 64*(1), 47–52.

Rodrigo, V., Krashen, S., & Gribbons, B. (2004). The effectiveness of two comprehensible-input approaches to foreign language instruction at the intermediate level. *System, 32*(1), 53.

Samway, K. D. (2006). *When English language learners write: Connecting research to practice, K-8.* Portsmouth, NH: Heinemann.

Van Staden, A. (2011). Put reading first: Positive effects of direct instruction and scaffolding for ESL learners struggling with reading. *Perspectives in Education, 29*(4), 10–21.

Virginia Board of Education. (2008). *History and social science standards of learning for Virginia public schools.* Richmond, VA: Virginia Department of Education.

Vygotsky, L. S. (1978). *Mind in society: The development of higher psychological processes.* Cambridge, MA: Harvard University Press.

Watts-Taffe, S., & Truscott, D. M. (2000). Focus on research using what we know about language and literacy development for ESL students in the mainstream classroom. *Language Arts, 77*(3), 258–265.

Williams, C., & Pilonieta, P. (2012). Using interactive writing instruction with kindergarten and first-grade English language learners. *Early Childhood Education Journal, 40*(3), 145–150.

Young, C., & Rasinski, T. V. (2013). Student-produced movies as a medium for literacy development. *Reading Teacher, 66*(8), 670–675.

Chapter Four

Literacy-Focused Science Instruction for Young English Learners

Carolyn Riley and Rodney Fitzgerald

Science instruction for English learners using "hands-on/minds-on" experiences fosters academic language development in the four language domains. The authors propose that literacy skills need to be embedded in science instruction through meaningful, purposeful planning. Readers will benefit from practical-scenario examples of what literacy-focused science instruction may look like, as well as recommendations, references, and supports that enrich ELs' academic language.

> Science is built up of facts as a house is of stones, but a collection of facts is no more a science than a pile of stones is a house. (Henri Poincare, *La Science et l'Hypothese*, 1908)

Funk and Rainie (2015) report, "79 percent of adults say that science has made life easier for most people and a majority is positive about science's impact on the quality of health care, food and the environment" (p. 1). However, the report from the Pew Research Center states that 46 percent of the American Association for the Advancement of Science (AAAS) scientists rank the U.S. K–12 science, technology, engineering, and mathematics (STEM) education as below average.

In addition, "75 percent of the AAAS scientists report that the lack of STEM education for K-12 is a major factor in the public's limited scientific knowledge potentially increasing the number of scientifically illiterate citizens in the future" (p. 2). The implication of this research for teachers is that both the public sector and the country's scientists believe that science is important for a quality life. However, scientists decry the lack of high-quality science teaching in the schools, suggesting that the publics' scientific literary will decrease in future generations.

Researchers know that children develop science understanding best when given multiple opportunities to engage in science exploration and experiences through inquiry (Bosse, Jacobs, & Anderson 2009; Gelman, Brenneman, Macdonald, & Roman, 2010). This allows them to see patterns, form theories, make predictions, consider alternate explanations, and build their experiential knowledge base.

Horizon Research (2012) has proposed that the key to effective science instruction appears to be setting up opportunities for students to engage with important science concepts and making sure that they make sense of these concepts through oral discourse and writing. Both oral discourse and written expression help all levels of English learners (ELs) construct the meaning of science academic vocabulary and concepts (Hudelson & Serna, 1994; Samway, 2006).

Teachers should also engage ELs in effective science instruction by incorporating literacy skills (Bialystock, 2008; Gee, 2008; Snow, 2008), developing the curiosities of students through the guided inquiry process (Amaral, Garrison, & Klentshy, 2002; Warren & Rosebery, 2008), and building on students' conceptual frameworks (García & Lee, 2008; Warren & Rosebery, 2008). These concepts are supported by the implementation of Jean Piaget's pioneering work in child development.

Piaget believed that internally generated knowledge eventually allows children to make their own discoveries and construct knowledge. Internally generated knowledge is earned by the learner through the creation of multiple experiences, questioning, and problem solving. The National Research Council (NRC) (1996) suggests that internally generated knowledge is developed for ELs when they pursue the integration of science, technology, engineering, art, and math (STEAM) learning in and out of the school setting.

Changing the acronym STEAM to STREAMS integrating science, technology, reading, engineering, art, mathematics, and social studies would add a needed literacy focus. Research has found that language learning and content-matter learning for ELs go hand in hand and should be taught at the same time (Cummins, 2000; Freeman & Freeman, 2001; Thomas & Collier, 1999). Academic instruction for ELs does not need to wait until the ELs have developed a high level of English proficiency (Herrera & Murry, 2016).

Cazden (1997) points out that language is learned because students want to interact with the world and the people in it. Teaching thematic units that use *overarching themes* or *big ideas* integrating as many of the content areas as possible advance the listening, speaking, reading, and writing skills of ELs. In this way students are able to academically interact with classmates and prepare for participation in the larger English-speaking community and world.

CHARACTERISTICS OF VOCABULARY INSTRUCTION FOR ELS

Research has drawn some surprising conclusions concerning the teaching of content-area vocabulary to ELs. For example, predicting words from context is a common practice employed by many elementary teachers. This works for students who are native speakers; however, Nation and Waring (2004) found that ELs often infer incorrect meanings because they may not know enough words in the passage to be able to comprehend the reading. Providing too much information too soon likewise confuses ELs. For instance, the word *table* can mean many things. There is the *table* where you can sit, the multiplication *table*, you can *table* a discussion, and the periodic *table*, to name a few. Learning all these meanings at once can put an EL on brain overload (Folse, 2004). Finally, there is the *exposure only* strategy. Miller and Gildea (1987) found that content vocabulary is difficult to learn by rote alone; effective instruction uses multiple strategies with academic vocabulary in context or associates the words with meaning that makes sense to ELs.

Krashen (2004) and Trelease (2006) suggest five strategies that develop permanent, in-depth content vocabulary for ELs. They are: (1) the development of word awareness, (2) teaching of important words directly, (3) analyzing and exploring words, (4) building learner control, and (5) expanding exposure. These strategies should happen daily, be frequent and brief, and involve active engagement (Levine & McCloskey, 2013).

The development of permanent in-depth literacy skills can be accomplished through inquiry-based science lessons. Once exposed to new academic vocabulary, ELs' word knowledge can be increased through expansion of content-area vocabulary via multiple and varied exposures throughout the day. Creating a rich classroom environment can develop word awareness of science vocabulary.

Analyzing and exploring science vocabulary can be skills added to instruction about word parts, their use and relationships. Likewise, discussion and read-alouds have the potential to expand literacy exposure when strategically used. At times teachers need to teach content words directly; these words should be chosen carefully and limited to the key concepts so as not to create mental overload for ELs (Levine & McCloskey (2013).

PRACTICAL APPLICATION FOR THE SCIENCE CLASSROOM

> A good scientist is a person in whom the childhood quality of perennial curiosity lingers on. Once he gets an answer, he has other questions. —Frederick Seitz

Science is important in everyone's daily life. We make multiple science-based decisions every day, from making healthy choices for meals to deciding whether to recycle or reuse an item in order to preserve resources. Students must have the curiosity to ask questions and the ability to pose the right problem (Graves, 2002). These are the skills that teachers should be teaching through the integration of science, technology, reading, engineering, art, mathematics, and social studies in order to prepare all students to be scientifically literate citizens in the twenty-first century.

Teachers are often confronted with the age-old question of how to balance the enormous amount of content they need to *cover* (science concepts and information dictated by standards and curriculum) and the short amount of time in which to present it, which may lead to a teaching frenzy. The reality is that teachers will never cover all the knowledge that students will need for their future.

Three factors are at work in teaching science. First, there is no way of knowing what specific *knowledge* students will need for their futures. For example, as a child you may have thought of a mouse as a small critter that sometimes got into your house. Teachers never could have anticipated that the word *mouse* would have an entirely different meaning in the future.

Second, knowledge continues to double at an increasingly faster and faster pace. Science knowledge grows by a factor of ten every fifty years so it should not be surprising that teachers are not able to cover all the knowledge that exists. Due to this vast amount of knowledge, it is becoming more and more difficult to decide what knowledge or facts students should learn. In fact, a new field called "knowledge management" has emerged so that organizations and companies can work more effectively with the vast amount of knowledge that now exists (Wang & Noe, 2010).

Third, facts change. For example, years ago teachers taught students that dinosaurs were cold-blooded. Scientists no longer believe that all dinosaurs were cold-blooded. In 2016, four elements were added to the Periodic Table. Pluto is now no longer a planet (or at least considered a dwarf planet by some). Which facts will you teach your students? It is very possible that what students learn in elementary school will become outdated by the time they reach adulthood.

Because of time constraints, some teacher may choose to embed science learning within the areas of reading and math. Students may read nonfiction science books to learn about science concepts yet this does not provide a rich deep understanding of formulating a hypothesis and experimentation with *hands-on/minds-on* discovery. When teachers teach science by only focusing on facts and gathering information through the reading of nonfiction books, they seriously limit students' abilities to become scientifically literate adults.

Students need to do what scientists do: investigate evidence through hands-on experiences, analyze data, discuss results with peers in large and small groups, then draw and publish conclusions. Students also need to learn that those conclusions can change with the presentation of new data. Rather than focus on facts, as teachers, it is our role to provide opportunities for students that spark student interest and build curiosity; these experiences should broaden and deepen students' science knowledge through observation, exploration, and experimentation, and expand purposefully designed learning environments to nurture students' natural curiosity of the world around them. These are integral skillsets students will need for their futures.

Like scientists, children are naturally curious. Curiosity is the natural cornerstone for learning. Science helps children find answers to their questions. It encourages them to ask why something happened and how things work. As Bernard Baruch said, "Millions of people saw the apple fall, but Newton asked why." Experiments and *hands-on/minds-on* activities in science feed this natural curiosity.

HANDS-ON MINDS-ON LEARNING

The impact of *hands-on/minds-on* component in science can be seen in an *a-ha* moment of a veteran teacher during a science workshop. Teachers were working with experiments on electricity in a science professional development workshop. They were asked to create a circuit that would light up a bulb: a lesson usually taught in third or fourth grade. After the lesson one teacher stated: "I could always explain how lighting the bulb worked, but I never understood it until now." This teacher's comment exemplifies the contrast between reading and exploring science ideas.

Scientists know the difference and the fact that inquiry learning requires exploration. Alexander Von Humboldt said, "I cannot live without experiments." As a scientist, he had to test out his theories. He had to explore and find out the whys. ELs need to explore in order to find answers to their questions and develop the academic vocabulary necessary to discuss those answers. Active exploration and vocabulary development happen for ELs when teachers create *hands-on/minds-on* science activities supported by rich classroom discourse and thoughtful written expression.

Language should be considered something to use and do things with rather than as content to be learned (Vygotsky, 1986). Teachers can support the language and vocabulary of ELs by providing a "content-rich and discourse-rich classroom environment" (Quinn, Lee, & Valdés, 2012, p. 1).

The Apple Lesson

Imagine a person who has never seen an apple. Someone tries to explain the properties of an apple to that person by using a photo of a red delicious apple. Based on the photo one could say the apple is red and shiny and infer that it is round, but one would not be able to use language to describe the properties of smell, touch, or taste. Next the person is shown a model of an apple. The model is about one inch in diameter (not the exact size of an average apple). The person can now touch the model of the apple but still cannot smell or taste it. The photo and the model help develop an understanding of an apple, but the person still does not have a complete understanding of an apple.

Finally, the person is given a red delicious apple. The person immediately notices the shiny texture of the apple's skin and the unique smell of the apple. As the apple is bitten into a crunchy sound is heard, and the person may notice a sweet juice coming from the apple. The senses of touch, taste, sight, smell, and hearing have been all engaged. The language used describes the properties of the apple from first-hand experiences rather than just reading about it or seeing a photo of an apple.

For example, at the beginning of a first-grade unit on rocks students often explore the properties of three rocks: tuft, scoria, and basalt. Tuft is a yellow, igneous rock of explosive volcanic eruption; scoria is a red variety of a type of lava; and basalt is a dark-colored, fine-grained, igneous rock. The first forty-five-minute lesson begins with an investigation of those three rocks. Students are engaged when looking at rocks that were so different from each other.

Students are asked to make a list of observations and vocabulary words that describe the three rocks. The words are posted in a pocket chart next to a sample of each rock. Then the questions generated by students are posted on a chart. Students can go to the classroom library to see what they could find out about the rocks. After this research, students can add answers to the questions that are posted. Then they can record findings from observations and from research in science journals.

If time is indeed a major factor preventing hands-on/minds-on experiences, consider rethinking the sequence of a unit already taught. During an insect unit, one teacher prepared students' background knowledge by reading about insects and asking students to fill in comprehension questions. This created a stressful situation for ELs who had not yet developed the concepts for the vocabulary being used.

One year the teacher simply changed the order of the unit. First, the students investigated the live insects. Students observed the insects, drew labeled pictures, discussed the characteristics, and conducted experiments with insects. The students were highly engaged, not only with the real insects but also with the packet information. The reality is that the packets did not build background knowledge but only provided information for students to memorize without providing the context.

Hands-on/minds-on experiences with the insects built the necessary background information the ELs needed to make sense of the packets of information about insects. This teacher did not use any more time than she always spent to teach the insect unit. In fact, the teacher reported that the students learned more scientific information in less time. It appears that everyone's time was used more efficiently by conducting the hands-on/minds-on experiences first.

Learning about Crickets

ELs need to practice language in collaboration with one another. A bilingual teacher saw language as a tool for meaning-making and communication (Vygotsky, 1986). The teacher knew that for kindergarten students, thinking develops as they use language to explore ideas and manipulate objects while negotiating meaning. The unit on insects provides an example of experiential language development.

The teacher introduced crickets by first asking the students to observe the crickets in a five-inch clear, closed tube. Leaves and sticks were placed in the tube to simulate habitat. One tube was placed at each table. Students gathered around and began talking about what they observed. Observations were recorded on a large chart. Next the students watched a YouTube video about crickets created by a fourth-grade student. More information was added to the chart.

Then the teacher used the Internet to bring up Sound Snap, asking students to listen to cricket sounds. Usually the classroom crickets would need a day or so to become acclimated to new environment before they began chirping. The teacher wanted to give students background knowledge of what cricket chirping sounded like. When the classroom crickets did start chirping the students knew immediately what they were hearing.

The teacher followed up by reading *The Very Quiet Cricket* by Eric Carle. The book ends with a cricket chirping. The students related to the chirping because they had first-hand knowledge of crickets chirping all day in the classroom. Throughout this study, the teacher recorded information about crickets citing the sources of the information: student YouTube video, personal observations of crickets, Eric Carle's book, and nonfiction books. At the end of the unit, students drew a cricket and wrote down what they learned in a data chart for a bilingual kindergarten (figure 4.1).

DEVELOPING OBSERVATION SKILLS THROUGH COMPARISON AND CONTRAST

A teacher at the sixth-grade level helped his ELs develop vocabulary and writing skills through observation and supporting frame sentences. He first instructed his students to set up a box T chart that they would use to compare and contrast wool and burlap.

The top rectangle of the box T chart (figure 4.2) listed the properties of wool and burlap that were the same. The bottom rectangle was divided into two sections to collect data on how the materials were different. The observa-

Information	Evidence
1. *Brincan*/jump	*El grillo estaba en la punta de una rama y luego saltó a la otra punta de la rama.* /the cricket was at the end of a branch and later jumped to the other end. *16 niños vieron que el grillo brincó.*/16 children saw the cricket jump
2. *Camina rápido*/walk quickly	*13 niños vieron que los grillos caminaban rápido de un lugar a otro.*/13 children saw that the crickets were walkin quickly from one place to another
3. *Hacen un sonido*/make a noise	Internet *había un sonido de grillos.*/ there was the sound of crickets Mrs. Smith *leyó un libro de grillos y sonido estaba ahí.*/read a book and the sound was there.

Figure 4.1. Data Chart for a Bilingual Kindergarten—Lo que sabemos de los grillos/What we know about crickets

tions were done in groups of four students to encourage oral discourse. After several minutes of observing and recording those observations, the teacher called the whole class together to create a comparison and contrast paragraph. He used a writing frame in order to provide structure to the paragraph. The writing frame followed this format:

The _____ and the _____ are the same because they both _____. In addition, they _____. They are different because the _____, and the _____.
Also_____
_____. Finally _____.

The whole class dictation resulted in this paragraph:

> The burlap and the wool are the same because they are both made of cloth and come from nature or living things. In addition, the burlap and the wool both have little squares for their shape and they are bendable and stretchable on the bias. They are both different because the burlap has a rough texture and the wool has a soft texture. Also, the burlap is a natural color and the wool has dyed threads. Finally, the burlap comes from a plant and the wool comes from an animal, the sheep.

In this case, the teacher used the science process skills of observing, measuring, and recording data; he used the language functions of describing, comparing, and contrasting information. The ELs were supported in their writing with a structured sentence frame. As the students became comfort-

Same	
Different	
Wool	Burlap

Figure 4.2. Box T Chart

able with the idea of comparing and contrasting information, the sentence frame was dropped so students did not become dependent on the structure.

Another teacher found a way to integrate science, literacy, self-assessment, and art. The lesson began by looking at twenty-five seemingly similar shells gathered in a pile. The number of shells should equal the number of students in the class. Students each had to select a shell and observe, measure, and record information about the shell. After several minutes, students were asked to put the shells back in the pile. Then they had to locate the shell using the descriptions and observations they had written.

This taught students the value of accurate recording of data. As a group, students discussed how detailed data about the shells could be accurately recorded so that another person could look at the data and locate the shell. Again, the shells were observed and more data recorded until finally notes were traded with a classmate. This time everyone successfully located the shell. Students discovered essential and useful information for note taking and data collection about the shells.

Part of the language arts curriculum required that students write descriptive paragraphs. This teacher integrated that skill and asked students to write a descriptive paragraph about their shells. Before students wrote the descriptive paragraphs, the class created a rubric about what features a descriptive paragraph should contain. Students then wrote their paragraphs describing their shells. Next, they put their shells back in the pile and traded paragraphs with a classmate. The students had to read the paragraph and find their partner's shell based on their partner's writing. Finally, students self-assessed their paragraphs based on the rubric that they had created.

By this time the students knew the shells intimately. The teacher then invited the art teacher to the classroom. The work of Georgia O'Keefe, a famous artist who created many paintings related to nature, was introduced. Students were asked to create a piece of art in the style of Georgia O'Keefe. This sequence of activities, as part of a larger unit, lent itself to incorporating strategies which develop and expand listening, speaking, reading, and writing skills for ELs.

A concern of many teachers is that ELs have a lack of background or prior knowledge that hinders their understanding of reading text. Embedding real science activities in the reading curriculum can easily develop background knowledge for ELs. One bilingual teacher worked with a story that involved yeast creating an explosion of a garbage can. The story could have been read and explained but instead the teacher brought a pop bottle to class, added yeast, sugar, and warm water; then the teacher attached a balloon to the top so the students could see the effect of the yeast. The students were fascinated and had many questions. The teacher transitioned into the story, suggesting that possibly some of the questions might be answered as the story was read. This simple experiment, found from a quick Internet search, piqued the curiosity of the ELs, in addition to building on conceptual frameworks.

All these examples emphasize that, in science, ELs learn language best when academic content is integrated with engaging and meaningful experiences. ELs should participate in classroom discourse focused on rich hands-on/minds-on activities and exciting academic content. ELs should have opportunities for extended engagement with complex ideas when focusing on both text and discourse. It is through integrated activities, classroom discourse, and purposeful engagement with complex ideas that ELs will develop the vocabulary and skills needed for the twenty-first century.

RECOMMENDATIONS FOR ACTION

1. *Do a time study of a week in your classroom.* Are you using all the time effectively? Is there any down time that could be used to do a science demonstration that would develop ELs' understanding of content-area vocabulary?
2. *Make a list of everyday materials that might be used to develop a concept in the reading stories from your curriculum.* For example, a teacher worked with the children's book *The Snowy Day* by Erza Jack Keats. The boy in the story spent the day exploring the snow. He put a snowball in his pocket, came in the house, and hung up his coat. In the morning, he was surprised that the snowball had melted. The teacher added science to this story by asking students to predict how long it would take a snowball to melt. The class went outside and made snowballs and conducted the experiment. This took about ten to fifteen minutes. The snowballs were put on the side counter and learning continued as planned. Every hour the class checked on the snowballs and recorded data. This built in a much-needed physical break (less

than five minutes per hour) for the students as well! In addition, they were observing, using language, and recording data.

After the data results were recorded, students had more questions such as: Does a snowball take longer to melt than loose snow? Is there a place in the room where snow would melt faster than other places? Is there a place in the room where we could slow down the melting? The class recorded these questions for future study. If, for some reason, a class was not allowed to go outside, then the teacher could gather up the snow in a five-gallon bucket, bring it in the classroom, make the snowballs, and create almost the same experience. The only thing that would be missing would be the children's experience and excitement of making their own snowball outside as the boy did in *The Snowy Day*.

3. If you live in an area where there is no snow, then find a book that uses materials from the environment in which you live. *Window* by Jeanne Baker is a wordless book that looks at the outside environment from one window. Students could observe and record the changes in the year through their own classroom windows. *The Tree* by Dana Lyons and David Danioth sends an environmental message from the perspective of an 800-year-old tree. Students could identify all the trees in their area, possibly leading to an in-depth study of one type of tree. Look in your classroom library for books whose content could be included in a science experience.

4. Other everyday materials can inexpensively help teachers develop the science process skills of observing, measuring, classifying, communicating, inferring, predicting, and experimenting. Consider using materials such as rocks and shells for sorting and classifying. Rocks and shells can also be used to teach the concept of the dichotomous key. Pinecones can lead to a seed investigation. Leaves in the fall can be used to develop classification skills. Classify them by colors or types of leaves. Add art by making a rubbing of the leaves.

5. *Read the current journals in science, social studies, and reading in order to keep abreast of new research regarding ELs.* Strategies such as KLEW (know, learned, evidence, wonder), interactive word walls, and mind maps are all effective for helping ELs develop vocabulary as well as learn scientific concepts. Science journals from National Science Teachers Association (NSTA) include *Science and Children* for elementary levels, *Science Scope* for middle school students, and *Science Teacher* for the secondary level. Social studies journals from National Council for Social Studies (NCSS) include *Social Studies and the Young Learner* and *Social Education* for elementary and *Middle Level Learning* for middle and high school. These journals include

lessons aligned with the Common Core Standards and include reading, writing, listening, and speaking strategies for all learners.

RESOURCES FOR SCIENCE CLASSROOMS

Materials about Crickets

- Mealworms for the insect study can be purchased at pet stores for under five dollars per one hundred.
- Tubes for crickets were found at the American Science Surplus at www.sciplus.com. Items are seasonal and vary, but usually something can be found that would work with the unit.
- Cricket sounds and wavelengths can be found at www.soundsnap/com/tags/cricket.

Teacher Resources

- This site hosts a video library for K–8 teachers; there are twenty-five half-hour videos with guides. The site can be found at http://learner.org/resources/series21.html.
- This site helps build teacher content in a variety of areas. The site can be found at www.learner.org/resources/browse.html?discipline=6.
- This site hosts a video library on inquiry teaching; there are nine videos ranging from twenty-five to fifty-five minutes in length. Guides are provided. The site can be found at www.learner.org/resources/series116.html.
- National Science Teachers Association provides articles, resources, standards, and professional journal publications. This site can be found at www.nsta.org.
- Learn about how your state might be updating K–12 science standards at www.nextgenscience.org.
- Lesson Plans—Kids' Science challenge. Fun educational science resources at various grade levels can be found at www.kidsciencechallenge.com.

CHILDREN'S BOOKS CITED

Baker, J. (1991). *The Window*. New York, NY: Greenwillow Books.
Carle, E. (1990). *The Very Quiet Cricket*. New York, NY: Philomel Books.
Keats, J. E. (1962). *The Snowy Day*. New York, NY: Viking Press.
Lyons, D., & Danioth, D. (2002). *The Tree*. Bellevue, WA: Illumination Arts.

REFERENCES

Amaral, O., Garrison, L., & Klentshy, M. (2002). Helping English language learners increase achievement through inquiry-based science instruction. *Bilingual Research Journal, 26*(2), 213–239.
Bialystok, E. (2008). Learning as a second language. In A. Rosebery & B. Warren (Eds.), *Teaching science to English language learners* (p. 107). Arlington, VA: NSTA Press.
Bosse, S., Jacobs, G., & Anderson, T. L. (2009). Science in the air. *Young Children, 64*, 10–15.
Cazden, C. B. (1997). Curriculum/language contents for bilingual education. In E. J. Briere (Ed.), *Language development in a bilingual setting* (pp. 129–138). Los Angeles, CA: California State University, National Dissemination and Assessment Center (ERIC Document Reproduction Service No. ED224661).
Cummins, J. (2000). This place nurtures my spirit: Creating contexts of empowerment in linguistically diverse schools. In R. Phillipson (Ed.), *Rights to language: Equity, power and education* (pp. 249–258). Mahwah, NJ: Lawrence Erlbaum.
Folse, K. S. (2004). *Vocabulary myths: Applying second language research to classroom teaching*. Ann Arbor, MI: University of Michigan Press.
Freeman, D. E., & Freeman, Y. S. (2001). *Between worlds: Access to second language acquisition* (2nd ed.) Portsmouth, NH: Heinemann.
Funk, C., & Rainie, L. (2015). Public and scientists' views on science and society. Pew Research Center. www.pewinternet.org/2015/01/29/public-and-scientists-views-on-science-and-society
Garcia, E., & Lee, O. (2008). Creating culturally responsive learning communities. In A. Rosebery & B. Warren (Eds.), *Teaching science to English language learners* (pp. 147–150). Arlington, VA: NSTA Press.
Gee, J. P. (2008). What is academic literacy? In A. Rosebery & B. Warren (Eds.), *Teaching science to English learners* (pp. 57–70). Arlington, VA: NSTA Press.
Gelman, R., Brenneman, K., Macdonald, G., & Roman., M. (2010). *Preschool pathways to science: Facilitating ways of thinking, talking, doing and understanding*. Baltimore: MD: Brookes Publishing.
Graves, D. H. (2002). *Testing is not teaching*. Portsmouth, NH: Heinemann.
Herrera, S. G., & Murry, K. G. (2016). *Mastering ESL/EFL methods* (3rd ed.). New York, NY: Pearson.
Horizon Research. (2012). 2012 national survey of science and mathematics educational highlights report. Retrieved on March 20, 2016, from www.horizon-research.com/2012-national-survey-of-science-and-mathematics-education-highlights-report-2
Hudelson, S. Y., & Serna, I. (1994). Beginning literacy in English in a whole-language bilingual program. In A. Flurkey & R. Meyer (Eds.), *Under the whole language umbrella: Many cultures, many voices* (pp. 278–294). Urbana, IL: National Teachers of English.
Krashen, S. (2004). *The power of reading*. Portsmouth, NH: Heinemann.
Lee, O., & Buxton, C. A. (2013). Integrating science and English proficiency for English language learners. *Theory into Practice, 52*(1), 36–42.
Levine, L. N., & McCloskey, M. L. (2013). *Teaching English language and content in mainstream classes: One class, many paths* (2nd ed.). New York, NY: Pearson.
Miller, G. A., & Gildea, P. M. (1987). How children learn words. *Scientific American, 257*(3), 94–97.
Nation, P., & Waring, R. (2004). *Second language reading and incidental vocabulary learning*. Retrieved on March 31, 2016, from www.robwaring.org/papers/various/waring_120304.pdf
National Research Council. (1996). *National Science Education Standards*. Washington, DC: National Academy Press.
Quinn, H., Lee, O., & Valdés, G. (2012) Language demands and opportunities in relation research. *Human Resource Magazine Review, 20*, 115–131. Retrieved on March 14, 2016, from www.elsevier.com/locate/humres
Samway, K. D. (2006). *When English language learners write: Connecting research to practice, K-8*. Portsmouth, NH: Heinemann.

Snow, C. (2008). What is the vocabulary of science? In A. Rosebery & B. Warren (Eds.), *Teaching science to English language learners* (pp. 71-84). Arlington, VA: NSTA Press.

Thomas, W. P., & Collier, V. P. (1999). Accelerated schooling for English language learners. *Educational Leadership, 56*(7), 46–49.

Trelease, J. (2006). *The read aloud handbook.* (6th ed.). New York, NY: Penguin Books.

Vygotsky, L. (1986). *Thought and language.* Cambridge, MA: MIT Press.

Wang, S., & Noe, R. (2010). Knowledge sharing: A review and direction for future research. *Human resource management review, 20*, 115–131.

Warren, B., & Rosebery, A. (2008). Using everyday experience to teach science. In A. Rosebery & B. Warren (Eds.), *Teaching science to English language learners* (pp. 39–50). Arlington, VA: NSTA Press.

Chapter Five

Supporting ELs in Learning to Write Scientifically

A Genre-Based Approach

Zhihui Fang, Brittany Adams, Cuiying Li, Caitlin Gallingane, Soowon Jo, Maureen Fennessy, and Suzanne Chapman

The centrality of writing to science learning and inquiry cannot be argued. The authors describe a powerful pedagogical framework for helping all students, and especially English learners, work to write scientifically while in the process of developing science literacy.

Science is widely recognized as a discipline that involves the empirical work of observing, manipulating, and experimenting with the material world. At the same time, however, it is also a form of discourse involving argument (Kuhn, 2010; Osborne, 2010). Scientists use language and other semiotic resources such as graphs, charts, pictures, diagrams, and sonograms to record, describe, classify, explain, model, and theorize the natural phenomena.

Scientists use evidence gathered from their reading, observation, and experiment to make their case for new ideas or alternative interpretations. These ideas or interpretations are in turn subjected to scrutiny and critique by the scientific community and the public. A study by Yore, Hand, and Florence (2004) found that scientists engage in many different types of writing—including journal articles, grant proposals, manuscript reviews, seminars, reports, essays, emails, lab notes, field notes, and lecture notes—in their daily work.

Given the centrality of writing to the conception of science and to the social practices of scientists, it is not surprising that the science education community has long embraced the view that writing should be an integral part of the K–12 science curriculum. In fact, writing is seen as not only an indispensable tool for doing science but also a powerful vehicle for learning science (Yore, 2004). It has been shown to enhance content understanding, promote conceptual change and inquiry, improve retention and learning, and cultivate scientific habits of mind (e.g., Chen, Hand, & McDowell, 2013; Key, Hand, Prain, & Collins, 1999; Rivard & Straw, 2000).

The National Research Council (2012, p. 42), in developing a framework for K–12 science education, identified eight science and engineering practices that are important for K–12 students to learn: asking questions and defining problems, developing and using models, planning and carrying out investigations, analyzing and interpreting data, using mathematics and computational thinking, constructing explanations and designing solutions, engaging in argument from evidence, and obtaining/evaluating/communicating information.

These practices are "language intensive" (Lee, Quinn, & Valdes, 2013, p. 2), requiring students to write and visually represent—along with other activities such as speaking, listening, reading, and viewing—as they develop models, present ideas, offer explanations, and engage in evidence-based reasoning and argumentation. Thus, if students are to develop as scientifically literate individuals, they must simultaneously develop facility in writing.

Despite the importance of writing to science inquiry and science learning, most science classrooms offer limited opportunities for students to write; and when they do write, very little support is provided by the teacher. In a recent study of English language learners' (ELs) writing experience in sixth-grade science classrooms, Qi (2015) found that students engaged in very little writing and that nearly 90 percent of their writing was less than one paragraph long, with filling in blanks, multiple choice answers, vocabulary worksheets, and short-answer questions being the most dominant forms of writing assignments. She further reported that although the science teachers believed in the importance of writing to science learning, they did not consider writing within the realm of their instructional responsibilities, rarely provided explicit instruction on science writing, and held lower expectations for ELs than for mainstream students.

Due in part to the lack of writing and writing instruction, many students, especially ELs, face challenges in science writing. For example, de Oliveira and Lan (2014) found that a "typical" fourth-grade EL, who easily conversed with his classroom peers and wrote narratives and personal stories in English language arts, experienced difficulty writing science experiment procedural recounts. Specifically, the EL struggled to use field-specific vocabulary, describe technical processes, and use clear temporal connectors to indicate sequences of events. Schleppegrell (1998) analyzed *descriptive reports* written by seventh- and eighth-grade students describing an image in their textbook. She observed that many of the ELs in the study failed to grasp the conventional genre features of description in science writing, such as generic participants, timeless verbs in simple present tense, and a large percentage of *being* and *having* clauses. Students exhibited multiple issues in attempting to negotiate the descriptive process. Grammatically, they struggled with subject-verb agreement, especially when using third-person singular and plural subjects, absent or inconsistent plural marking, possessive marking, and tense marking.

In terms of register, students in Schleppegrell's study (1998) failed to decontextualize their description to situate the observation as timeless and generic. Students frequently provided excessive interpersonal context through choice of tense, point of view, and choice of finite verbs. They also struggled to maintain cohesive pronominal references when describing animals in their selected photos, switching between pronouns such as *it* and *he*. Overall, while the students were comfortable with the concept of description, they experienced challenges in producing register features typical of the science description genre, relying on a limited number of lexical resources to relay their observations (e.g., mostly sticking to commonly occurring attributes like *big, short, fat,* etc.).

Seah, Clark, and Hart (2011) focused on the genre of explanation, analyzing texts written by seventh-grade ELs on the scientific phenomenon of expansion. Their analysis revealed that students did not share a common understanding of what constitutes a scientific explanation. Specifically, students were limited in their use of lexical resources to *explain* the concept of expansion, frequently using scientific terms in such ambiguous ways that the researchers could not determine if the term was being utilized in the scientific or practical sense. Additionally, almost all the students used *it* as an indiscriminate pronoun in such a way that it was often impossible to determine what object or concept *it* was referencing. However, most students were able to recognize a cause-and-effect pattern within the expansion activity, indicating that students likely grasped the concept of expansion, but were unable to communicate their knowledge appropriately.

Taken together, extant research suggests that science writing is a linguistically and cognitive demanding task and that many ELs lack the language resources for making scientific meaning in genre-specific and register-appropriate ways. As shown in Text 1 (see text 1), a science report written by a seventh-grade EL, these students tend to draw on the grammatical resources of everyday spontaneous speech in academic and disciplinary writing—such as interrogative sentences (e.g., *Have you ever wondered what makes an alligator so cool?*), colloquial expressions (*well; so cool; actually; the cool thing about being a reptile is . . . ; that is cool; so much; really cool*), and reference to personal thought processes (e.g., *I think, I know*)—resulting in writing that sounds more interpersonal and less authoritative.

These students' responses are contrary to the more objective, formal, and assertive stance often found in science reports, where scientists develop complex chains of reasoning through the use of long noun phrases, nominalizations, zig-zagging referential structures, connectors that serve specific roles, and logical metaphors (Fang & Schleppegrell, 2008). Common school-based science genres include procedural recounts, research articles, demonstrations, field studies, reports, and explanations (Christie & Derewianka, 2008). Each of these genres calls for a particular constellation and calibration of lexical and grammatical choices, which are quite distinct from those used in everyday social interactions. It is thus critical that teachers incorporate explicit discussion of lexical, grammatical, and discursive resources into their presentations of science topics and writing instruction to help students understand how language choices convey different meanings for different purposes and across different contexts.

Text 1 (Alligator)
Have you ever wondered what makes an alligator so cool? Well they are reptiles. They are actually not the same as crocodiles and they are carnivores. The cool thing about being a reptile is because they are so much different than other animals. That is cool. They are different than crocodiles. Crocodiles have pointed snouts and are smaller. Alligators have round snouts and are bigger. Alligators are carnivores. They eat meat like fish, dogs, chickens and have killed humans. They are scary. I know they are scary, but still they are amazing creatures. I think they are really cool. (Written by a seventh-grade ELL)

A GENRE-BASED APPROACH

One way to get this job done is the Sydney School Genre-Based Pedagogy, or SGP (Rose & Martin, 2012). First developed in Australia as a response to the prevalence of a process approach that emphasizes the planning-drafting-composing-revising-editing-publishing framework, SGP focuses on the linguistic resources students need to write effective and relevant texts, offering explicit, systematic explanations of how language choices present information, embed perspective, and structure text in ways that are specific to particular genres, disciplines, or contexts.

SGP foregrounds the role of teachers as more knowledgeable others in providing support to students in ways that raise their awareness and understanding of how and why a text means what it means and why a text is more or less effective for its own purpose. According to Hyland (2007, p. 150), SGP has the following features:

- Explicit: makes clear what is to be learned to facilitate the acquisition of writing skills
- Systematic: provides a coherent framework for focusing on both language and contexts
- Needs-based: ensures that course objectives and content are derived from students' needs
- Supportive: gives teachers a central role in scaffolding students' learning and creativity
- Empowering: provides access to the patterns and possibilities of variation in valued texts
- Critical: provides the resources for students to understand and challenge valued discourses
- Consciousness-raising: increases teachers' awareness of texts to confidently advise students on writing

SGP can be implemented in four phases: building knowledge and context, analyzing text, jointly constructing text with the teacher, and independently constructing text. In phase 1, students develop content knowledge about the topic they are going to write about through reading and discussing texts in the target genre. At the same time, they also gain a sense of the cultural and situational contexts of the genre under study. In phase 2, mentor texts in the target genre are selected and analyzed, with particular attention to the purpose of the text as well as how the generic structure of the text and its lexical and grammatical features contribute to achieving that purpose. In phase 3, the teacher and students construct a text in the target genre together, with the teacher acting as a scribe, writing and, when necessary, rewording students' contributions on the board. When students are confident enough about the specific characteristics of the genre, they move to phase 4, when they write on their own, incorporating and recontextualizing the language choices that are appropriate for the genre.

To illustrate how the above process works, we describe below how a sixth-grade science teacher, Mrs. Jones, engages her students in learning to write the biography genre as part of their nine-week unit on scientists and their careers. The science curriculum for the grade also includes three additional units: generating problems for scientific investigation, finding solutions to the problem through experiments, and project-based exploration of science-related issues.

The overall goal of the curriculum is for students to develop interest in science, enhance understanding of the nature of science, and acquire scientific knowledge and habits of mind. The unit on exploration of scientists and their careers specifically aims at developing students' understanding of science as a human enterprise interdependent with culture, society, and history.

The culminating project for the unit involves writing a biography of a scientist in whom students are interested.

To prepare students for the culminating project, Mrs. Jones immerses her students in reading and discussing many biographies of famous scientists, especially those of women and from minority backgrounds. Science biographies present life stories of scientists, highlighting their key accomplishments as well as personal and professional attributes that contribute to their success. As such, they are ideal resources for helping students develop an appreciation of the nature of science (e.g., science is a human endeavor; science is not just for the genius; science is not always clean and unequivocal; scientific knowledge is subject to change).

To ensure that her students have ample science biographies to read, Mrs. Jones applies for a school grant that provides funds for her to purchase some forty-five quality science biographies she has identified from the annual lists of outstanding science trade books for K–12 students compiled by the National Science Teachers Association (www.nsta.org). She also checks out roughly three dozen science biographies from her school and local libraries. As a result, her classroom library has a rich collection of biographies that covers a range of time periods, fields of study, and ethnic and gender groups. A sampling of this collection can be found in textbox below.

Sample Science Biographies Used in Sixth Grade
- Aczel, A. D. (2003). *Pendulum: Léon Foucault and the triumph of science.* New York, NY: Atria Books.
- Aldrin, B. (2005). *Reaching for the moon.* New York, NY: HarperCollins.
- Birch, B. (2000). *Marie Curie: Courageous pioneer in the study of radioactivity.* Woodbridge, CT: Blackbirch Press.
- Brown, D. (2004). *Odd boy out: Young Albert Einstein.* Boston, MA: Houghton Mifflin.
- Burleigh, R. (2003). *Into the woods: John James Audubon lives his dream.* New York, NY: Atheneum.
- Busby, P. (2002). *First to fly: How Wilbur & Orville Wright invented the airplane.* New York, NY: Crown.
- Dash, J. (2006). *A dangerous engine: Benjamin Franklin, from scientist to diplomat.* New York, NY: Frances Foster Books.
- Davies, J. (2004). *The boy who drew birds: A story of John James Audubon.* Boston, MA: Houghton Mifflin.
- Di Domenico, K. (2002). *Super women in science.* Toronto, ON: Second Story Press.
- Editors of Time for Kids with Lisa deMauro. (2005). *Thomas Edison: A brilliant inventor.* New York, NY: HarperCollins.
- Ehrlich, A. (2003). *Rachel: The story of Rachel Carson.* San Diego, CA: Harcourt.
- Fleischman, J. (2002). *Phineas Gage: A gruesome but true story about brain science.* Boston, MA: Houghton Mifflin.

- Fleming, C. (2003). *Ben Franklin's almanac: Being a true account of the good gentleman's life.* New York, NY: Atheneum.
- Fradin, D. B. (2006). *With a little luck: Surprising stories of amazing discoveries.* New York, NY: Dutton.
- Hines, G. (2005). *Midnight forests: A story of Gifford Pinchot and our national forests.* Honesdale, PA: Boyds Mills Press.
- Hopping, L. J. (2005). *Bone detective: The story of forensic anthropologist Diane France.* Washington, D.C.: J. Henry Press.
- Hulls, J. (2003). *Rider in the sky: How an American cowboy (Samuel Cody) built England's first airplane.* New York, NY: Crown.
- Johnson, D. (2006). *Onward: A photobiography of African-American polar explorer Matthew Henson.* Washington, D.C.: National Geographic.
- Jones, L. (2000). *Five brilliant scientists.* New York, NY: Scholastic.
- Krull, K. (2005). *Leonardo da Vinci.* New York, NY: Viking.
- Krull, K. (2006). *Isaac Newton.* New York, NY: Viking.
- Lasky, K. (2003). *The man who made time travel (John Harrison).* New York, NY: Melanie Kroupa Books.
- Lasky, K. (2006). *John Muir: America's first environmentalist.* Cambridge, MA: Candlewick Press.
- Lawson, K. (2003). *Darwin and evolution for kids: His life and ideas, with 21 activities.* Chicago, Il.: Chicago Review Press.
- MacDonald, F. (2000). *Albert Einstein: Genius behind the theory of relativity.* Woodbridge, CT: Blackbirch Press.
- MacLeod, E. (2003). *Albert Einstein: A life of genius.* Toronto, ON: Kids Can Press.
- MacLeod, E. (2004). *Marie Curie: A brilliant life.* Toronto, ON: Kids Can Press.
- McClafferty, C. (2006). *Something out of nothing: Marie Curie and radium.* New York, NY: Farrar, Straus and Giroux.
- McCully, E. A. (2006). *Marvelous Mattie: How Margaret K. Knight became an inventor.* New York, NY: Farrar, Straus and Giroux.
- Pasachoff, N. (2003). *Niels Bohr: Physicist and humanitarian.* Berkeley Heights, NJ: Enslow Publishers.
- Patent, D. H. (2001). *Charles Darwin: The life of a revolutionary thinker.* New York, NY: Holiday House.
- Ray, D. K. (2004). *The flower hunter: William Bartram, America's first naturalist.* New York, NY: Farrar, Straus and Giroux.
- Richard, O. (2002). *African American women scientists and inventors.* New York, NY: Wiley.
- Robbins, L. E. (2001). *Louis Pasteur and the hidden world of microbes.* New York, NY: Oxford University Press.
- Ross, M. E. (2000). *Exploring the earth with John Wesley Powell.* Minneapolis, MN: Carolrhoda Books.
- Ross, M. E. (2000). *Pond watching with Ann Morgan.* Minneapolis, MN: Carolrhoda Books.
- Shell, B. (2005). *Sensational scientists: The journeys and discoveries of 24 men and women of science.* Vancouver, BC: Raincoast Books.
- Todes, D. (2000). *Ivan Pavlov: Exploring the animal machine.* New York, NY: Oxford University Press.

With her classroom library well stocked with science biographies, Mrs. Jones decides to set up a home science reading program that motivates her students to read and discuss what they read with peers every week. Before the program starts, she sends out a letter to the parent or guardian of every student, explaining the program and encouraging them to support their children reading at home.

Each Wednesday, students in Mrs. Jones's classroom check out one book from the classroom library to read. They can read the book on their own or with their family members (e.g., sibling, parent/guardian, friend). As students read, they are expected to document in a graphic organizer the process of scientific inquiry in which the scientist sensed a problem, made hypotheses, conducted experiments, evaluated the findings, and presented/published his/her work. They also identify any significant historical events that helped shape the scientist's work and key scientific attitudes exemplified by the scientist (e.g., curiosity, open-mindedness, flexibility, reflectiveness, skepticism, demand for accuracy and precision, accepting ambiguity, risk taking, perseverance, and respect for evidence). They then share what they have learned about their scientist, science inquiry, and science career, as well as things they wonder about, in class each Wednesday (before checking out a new book), sometimes with small groups and other times with the whole class.

Recognizing that many of her students, including ELs, are not familiar with the biography genre, Mrs. Jones conducts a close reading session once a week, when she engages her students in detailed analysis of either a brief passage or a short essay in the genre. During close reading, she reads the text aloud and initiates a discussion about the purpose of the text, its schematic structure, its lexical and grammatical features, and the qualities of a good biography.

In one lesson, Mrs. Jones notes that a good biography is well-researched and well-written, meaning that the author has conducted research on the scientist and the type of science involved and validated findings with multiple sources. She asks students to read the jacket page of each book (or simply Google the author) so that they gain a sense of what the author's credentials are and whether s/he has conducted the necessary background research (e.g., interviews, archive research, document analysis, site visits) before writing the biography.

In other lessons, Mrs. Jones focuses on the purpose, structure, and linguistic features of biography. She points out to students that a biography tells the life story of a significant historical figure, often highlighting important moments or turning points in the person's life. She shows students that a biography covers a wide span of time, typically organized around early experience, career, and later life. She further explains that a good science biography typically contains an orientation that provides a synopsis of the scientist's life and significant contributions, a sequence of events that chronicles key moments in the scientist's life, and an evaluation that assesses the scientist's legacy.

To make her points more concrete, Mrs. Jones chooses a biography about Alice Hamilton (see Text 2), a physician and a leading authority on lead poisoning and industrial diseases, as a mentor text. *Mentor text*, sometimes called *anchor text*, refers to any piece of writing (e.g., book, article, passage) that can be used as a good example of its genre to teach students about aspects of a writer's craft, such as a specific strategy, skill, or style of writing (Dorfman & Cappelli, 2009). Using the mentor text, Mrs. Jones engages her students in discussing questions such as (a) what is the purpose of the text? (b) how is that purpose achieved? (c) who wrote the text? (d) how was the text written? and (e) who is the intended audience of the text?

Mrs. Jones might ask students how the structure of Text 2 helps achieve the overall purpose of the text, which is to report on Hamilton's life and scientific contributions in an informative way. She notes that Text 2 consists of three parts, each contributing to the overall purpose of the text. The first paragraph is an orientation that introduces Hamilton and summarizes her career and major scientific accomplishments. The second and third paragraphs present key moments in the scientist's life and career. The last paragraph states the legacy of Hamilton's scientific contributions.

Text 2 (Biography of Alice Hamilton)
Alice Hamilton was born in New York City on February 27, 1869. A pioneer in industrial toxicology and a nonconformist who valued personal liberty above all else, Hamilton became a leading American authority on lead poisoning and one of the handful of worldwide specialists on industrial diseases by 1916. Her reports on lead, and later on rubber and munitions, led to improved safety standards nationwide.
The daughter of a successful grocer, Alice Hamilton chose medicine as a career as a means to be both independent and socially useful. Her sister, Edith Hamilton, chose a different path, becoming a well-known classics scholar and author. Alice spent more than a decade as a resident of Chicago's famous settlement house, Hull House. She developed her friendship with reformer Jane Addams there, and also began to combine her scientific research skills with her latent reformist zeal.
Focusing on industrial diseases, Alice Hamilton became a special investigator for the U.S. Bureau of Labor in 1911. She broke the gender barrier by becoming the first woman on the faculty of Harvard University in 1919 and later its first professor of public health. During the course of her long career, Hamilton published numerous studies on industrial toxicology, several books, and an autobiography.
Alice Hamilton died on September 22, 1970, in Hadlyme, Connecticut. In tribute to her work, the National Institute for Occupational Safety and Health presents awards in her name to those scientists and engineers who excel in the field.

Source: www.biography.com/people/alice-hamilton-9326498.

Besides the discussion about the generic structure of the text, Mrs. Jones also deconstructs some sentences that are unfamiliar to students, especially ELs. She focuses on the appositive, nonfinite clause, and embedded clause, each in a separate mini-lesson lasting ten to fifteen minutes, as these three grammatical features are present in Text 2 and they all serve the same function (i.e., adding more information to the sentence). Because her ELs' writing is often choppy and speech-like, she feels that these three grammatical resources are perfect for showing students how information can be packaged in ways that make their writing more compact and scientific.

In her lesson on the appositive, Mrs. Jones writes the following two sentences from Text 2 on board, with the appositive phrase highlighted:

- Her sister, *Edith Hamilton*, chose a different path, becoming a well-known classics scholar and author.
- *The daughter of a successful grocer*, Alice Hamilton chose medicine as a career as a means to be both independent and socially useful.

She tells students that "Edith Hamilton" and "the daughter of a successful grocer" are both called, grammatically, the appositive in that each is a noun phrase separated by a comma from the rest of the sentence and used to provide more information about another noun (or noun phrase) immediately preceding (*her sister*) or following (*Alice Hamilton*) it. She points out that the added information could have been expressed with a complete sentence (e.g., Edith Hamilton is Alice Hamilton's sister; Alice Hamilton is the daughter of a successful grocer), separate from the original sentence, but that in doing so the added information, which may be neither essential to nor the focus of the article, becomes foregrounded and disrupts the flow of the text.

Mrs. Jones explains that scientists often use grammatical resources like the appositive to make their writing more compact and informative. Sensing that her students have understood the concept of the appositive and its functionality, she then asks them to search for more examples of the appositive in Text 2. Students have no trouble coming up with the following examples (the appositive is italicized):

- *A pioneer in industrial toxicology and a nonconformist who valued personal liberty above all else*, Hamilton became a leading American authority on lead poisoning and one of the handful of worldwide specialists on industrial diseases by 1916.

- Alice spent more than a decade as a resident of Chicago's famous settlement house, *Hull House*.

The students also turn each appositive into a complete sentence, discussing how the transformation impacts the flow and meaning of the text. To reinforce students' understanding of the appositive, Mrs. Jones has her students search for more examples of the appositive in other texts they have been reading and later complete a worksheet that involves turning a sentence with the appositive into two complete sentences, or conversely, turning two full sentences into one sentence with an appositive.

In follow-up lessons, Mrs. Jones introduces the concepts of embedded clause (i.e., a group of words with a subject and a verb that constitute part of a noun or noun phrase) and nonfinite clause (i.e., a clause whose verb does not show tense [because it is in *-ing* or *-ed* form] and whose subject is missing but can be inferred from the subject of the main clause), showing students how these two grammatical resources are also functional in integrating two possible sentences into one sentence without losing information. Examples of nonfinite clauses and embedded clauses from Text 2 (see below) and other texts are identified and discussed. Students also complete exercises that require them to turn (a) nonfinite clause or embedded clause into a complete sentence or (b) two sentences into one sentence with a nonfinite or embedded clause, and discuss how the change impacts both the meaning and the discursive flow of the text.

Sentences with Embedded Clauses from Text 2

- A pioneer in industrial toxicology and a nonconformist *who valued personal liberty above all else*, Hamilton became a leading American authority on lead poisoning and one of the handful of worldwide specialists on industrial diseases by 1916.
- In tribute to her work, the National Institute for Occupational Safety and Health presents awards in her name to those scientists and engineers *who excel in the field*.

Sentences with Non-Finite Clauses from Text 2

- *Focusing on industrial diseases*, Alice Hamilton became a special investigator for the United States Bureau of Labor in 1911.
- Her sister, Edith Hamilton, chose a different path, *becoming a well-known classics scholar and author*.

Having read and discussed many different scientists for the first five weeks of the unit, the class is now ready to start thinking about the scientist on whom they want to focus. Mrs. Jones has her students identify at least three sources (books or articles) they would use in writing the biography of their favorite scientist. As students read their sources, they take careful notes of key events in the scientist's life, the social-economic-historical-political contexts of his/her discovery or invention, the particular scientific attitude(s) exemplified in the biography, and the significance of his/her scientific contributions.

To model the writing process for the six ELs in her class, Mrs. Jones decides to practice writing a biography with them, with her acting as a scribe writing sentences contributed by the students. Together, they select a scientist they have all read about and discussed. They then jointly plan and write the orientation paragraph that introduces the scientist and highlights his or her contributions. Next, Mrs. Jones divides the students into three groups of two. Each group is responsible for developing an assigned topic sentence into one paragraph that describes one key event or accomplishment in the scientist's life or one scientific attitude exemplified by the scientist.

As each group contributes their paragraph, sentence by sentence, for Mrs. Jones to scribe on a piece of chart paper, the teacher and the other two groups make comments and wording changes (when appropriate) to improve the assembled text. The three groups then jointly construct the concluding paragraph that evaluates the legacy of the scientist's discovery or invention.

The last two weeks of the unit are dedicated to independent writing. Mrs. Jones has students complete a draft biography of their favorite scientist outside class. They then bring their drafts to class for self- and peer editing, using the checklist provided in the following textbox.

Checklist for Science Biography Writing
- Is the purpose of my biography clear?
- Is my biography interesting and informative?
- Is the information presented in the text accurate and factual?
- Does my biography include an orientation, a sequence of three key events (or major accomplishments), and an evaluation?
- What scientific attitude is exemplified in my biography?
- Do I draw on at least three sources in my writing? Are my sources reliable?
- Do I avoid using colloquial expressions or subjective language?
- Does each paragraph include a topic sentence with supporting details?
- Is the transition between paragraphs smooth?
- Do I use visuals in my writing? If so, are they well integrated with the rest of the text?
- Do I use correct grammar, punctuation, and spelling?

This is followed by a teacher-student conference to improve the drafts, with particular attention to the assignment checklist. The first and final drafts of one EL's writing appear in table 5.1. Mrs. Jones organizes an "author tea party" on the final day of the unit, where students present their final drafts to their peers and invited guests (parents). The polished biographies are also published in a class monograph that students bring home to share with their families.

First Draft	Final Draft
Have you ever heard of Dr. Charles R. Drew? Well you should know him if you donated blood. If you haven't let me tell you a little bit about him. He was a black scientist born on June 3, 1904 in Washington, D.C., star-football player, made the first blood bank, and a mystery about his death. The first fact about him was that he was good in sports. He was the star-football player and was the captain of his football team. He was an all-American half-back. He was also awarded 20 medals. He later became the director of athletes at Mogen State University. He had a good education. He was smart because he graduated with honors. The second fact about Dr. Drew was that He got his Medical Doctorate (M.D.) Master of Surgery (C.M.) and Doctor of Science. He wanted to serve mankind by preserving blood. He made the first blood bank by preserving blood for WWII victims. He utilized his techniques and made the Red Cross. He became Professor of Surgery and Chief Surgery. The last fact is how long he had lived. He was born in 1904 and died when he was hit by a car in 1950. Many believed he died from discrimination because he was a black man. This is the facts about the life and accomplishments of Dr. Charles R. Drew. Without his hard work we would not be able to save lives.	Dr. Charles R. Drew is an African American scientist who made the first blood bank. He was awarded twenty medals for his accomplishments. Dr. Drew had a good education and a successful career. He graduated from Amherst College with honors. He went on to get his Master of Surgery and Doctor of Medicine degrees. He later became a professor of surgery at Howard University and chief surgeon at Freedmen's Hospital. Wanting to serve mankind by preserving blood, he developed a method for processing and preserving blood without cells. He made the first blood bank by preserving blood for WWII victims. At the same time, he also fought against the racist policy of segregating the blood donated by African Americans. Dr. Drew was also good at sports. He was a star football player. An all-American halfback in college, he was captain of his football team. He later became the director of athletes at Morgan State University before enrolling in medical school. Dr. Drew was born in 1904 in Washington, D.C. He died in 1950 when he was hit by a car in Alabama. His death remains a mystery to date. Many believe he died from discrimination because he was a Black man. These are the facts about the life and accomplishments of Dr. Charles R. Drew. Without his hard work, we would not be able to save lives. References • Haber, L. (1970). *Black pioneers of science and invention*. New York, NY: Harcourt, Brace & World. • Schraff, A. (2003). *Dr. Charles Drew: Blood bank inventor*. Berkeley Heights, NJ: Enslow. • Trice, L. (2000). *Charles Drew: Pioneer of blood plasma*. New York, NY: McGraw-Hill. • https://en.wikipedia.org/wiki/Charles_R._Drew

CONCLUSION

Writing is both a tool for learning subject matter and an integral part of disciplinary social practice. Despite its importance in subject-area learning, it is the most neglected R (the other two being reading and arithmetic) in the school curriculum (Graham & Perin, 2007). Once past the formative reading and writing instruction of the K–3 years, students are expected to be able to apply those skills for more complex learning in the subject areas. By then, teachers often assume that the necessary foundational language and literacy skills for negotiating content-area language and writing have already been acquired.

Even when teachers do recognize that texts in content areas like science are more demanding to write than everyday texts, they often assume that mere exposure to these texts will enable students to learn to navigate disciplinary language over time. What needs to be recognized is that content-area writing in general and science writing in particular present a significant challenge to many ELs. One main reason for the challenge is that these ELs lack the linguistic tools for making scientific meanings in ways expected by school.

To develop their competence in science writing, students need ample opportunities to read and write texts in the discipline for authentic purposes (Kohnen, 2013); they also need explicit guidance in how language (and other semiotic) choices construct text and communicate scientific meanings in genre-specific and discipline-appropriate ways (Fang, 2010). An evidence-based approach for accomplishing these goals is the Sydney School Genre-Based Pedagogy (SGP), described in this chapter.

RESOURCES FOR TEACHERS

Listed below are several resources that teachers will find relevant and useful as they begin to implement the approach in the context of science learning.

- de Oliveira, L., & Iddings, J. (2014). *Genre pedagogy across the curriculum: Theory and application in U.S. classrooms and contexts*. London, UK: Equinox.
- Fang, Z. (2010). *Language and literacy in inquiry-based science classrooms, Grades 3-8*. Thousand Oaks, CA: Corwin Press; Arlington, VA: NSTA Press
- Fang, Z., & Schleppegrell, M. J. (2008). *Reading in secondary content areas: A language-based pedagogy*. Ann Arbor, MI: University of Michigan Press.

- Hyland, K. (2004). *Genre and second language writing.* Ann Arbor, MI: University of Michigan.
- Pytash, K. E., & Ferdig, R. E. (2014). *Exploring technology for writing and writing instruction.* Hershey, PA: IGI Global.
- Rose, D., & Martin, J. (2012). *Learning to write/reading to learn: Genre, knowledge and pedagogy in the Sydney School.* Bristol, CT: Equinox.
- Stead, T., & Hoyt, L. (2012). *A guide to teaching nonfiction writing.* Portsmouth, NH: Heinemann.

REFERENCES

Chen, Y-C., Hand, B., & McDowell, L. (2013). The effects of writing-to-learn activities on elementary students' conceptual understanding: Learning about force and motion through writing to older peers. *Science Education, 97*(5), 745–771.

Christie, F., & Derewianka, B. (2008). *School discourse: Learning to write across the years of schooling.* London, UK: Continuum.

de Oliveira, L., & Iddings, J. (2014). *Genre pedagogy across the curriculum: Theory and application in U.S. classrooms and contexts.* London, UK: Equinox.

de Oliveira, L., & Lan, S. (2014). Writing science in an upper elementary classroom: A genre-based approach to teaching English language learners. *Journal of Second Language Writing, 25,* 23–29.

Dorfman, L. R., & Cappelli, R. (2009). *Nonfiction mentor texts.* Portland, ME: Stenhouse.

Fang, Z. (2010). *Language and literacy in inquiry-based science classrooms, Grades 3-8.* Thousand Oaks, CA: Corwin Press; Arlington, VA: NSTA Press

Fang, Z., & Schleppegrell, Z. (2008). *Reading in secondary content areas: A language-based pedagogy.* Ann Arbor, MI: University of Michigan Press.

Graham, S., & Perin, D. (2007). *Writing next: Effective strategies to improve writing of adolescents in middle and high schools.* Washington, DC: Alliance for Excellent Education.

Hyland, K. (2004). *Genre and second language writing.* Ann Arbor, MI: University of Michigan.

Hyland, K. (2007). Genre pedagogy: language, literacy and L2 writing instruction. *Journal of Second Language Writing, 16,* 148–164.

Key, C., Hand, B., Prain, V., & Collins, S. (1999). Using the science writing heuristic as a tool for learning from laboratory investigations in secondary science. *Journal of Research in Science Teaching, 36*(10), 1065–1084.

Kohnen, A. (2013). The authenticity spectrum: The case of a science journalism writing project. *English Journal, 102*(5), 28–34.

Kuhn, D. (2010). Teaching and learning science as argument. *Science Education, 94,* 810–824.

National Research Council. (2012). *A framework for K-12 science education: Practices, crosscutting concepts, and core ideas.* Washington, DC: The National Academies Press.

Lee, O., Quinn, H., & Valdes, G. (2013). Science and language for English language learners in relation to Next Generation Science Standards and with implications for Common Core State Standards for English Language Arts and Mathematics. *Educational Researcher, 20*(10), 1–11.

Osborne, J. (2010). Arguing to learn in science: The role of collaborative, critical discourse. *Science, 328,* 463–466.

Pytash, K. E., & Ferdig, R. E. (2014). *Exploring technology for writing and writing instruction.* Hershey, PA: IGI Global.

Qi, Y. (2015). *Learning to write in science: A study of English language learners' writing experience in sixth-grade science classrooms.* Unpublished doctoral dissertation, University of Florida, Gainesville, Florida.

Rivard, L. P., & Straw, S. B. (2000). The effect of talk and writing on learning science: An exploratory study. *Science Education, 84*, 566–593.

Rose, D., & Martin, J. (2012). *Learning to write/reading to learn: Genre, knowledge and pedagogy in the Sydney School.* Bristol, CT: Equinox.

Schleppegrell, M. (1998). Grammar as resource: Writing a description. *Research in the Teaching of English, 32*(2), 182–209.

Seah, L., Clarke, D., & Hart, C. (2011). Understanding students' language use about expansion through analyzing their lexicogrammatical resources. *Science Education, 95*(5), 852–876.

Stead, T., & Hoyt, L. (2012). *A guide to teaching nonfiction writing.* Portsmouth, NH: Heinemann.

Yore, L. (2004). Why do future scientists need to study the language arts? In W. Saul (Ed.), *Crossing borders in literacy and science: Perspectives on theory and practice* (71–107). Newark, DE: International Reading Association.

Yore, L., Hand, B., Florence, M. (2004). Scientists views of science, models of writing, and science writing practices. *Journal of Research in Science Teaching, 41*(4), 338–369.

Chapter Six

Student-Centered Approaches for Teaching Social Studies to English Learners

Mayra C. Daniel, Carolyn Riley, and Teresa Kruger

The study of history challenges English learners at both elementary and secondary levels. This reflects learners' unfamiliarity with historical events and, specifically, differences across students' funds of knowledge. The authors address issues that stem from the language requirements required in this discipline and the design of expository texts used in history education. They offer ideas to teachers that will engage students as they deconstruct the message in history texts.

English learners (ELs) are challenged to understand concepts in social studies classes because the content, vocabulary, and discourse patterns used in this discipline are often unfamiliar to them (de Oliveira, 2010). In addition to discipline-specific vocabulary and discourse patterns, social studies courses require much background knowledge about U.S. history and culture. Students who do not have this knowledge may not be able to access a curriculum that has been developed for native English speakers (Misco & Castañeda, 2009).

The knowledge that ELs bring to school related to their country's history and political system is often very different from the democratic model in place in the United States. Therefore, it is imperative that teachers investigate learners' histories and explore teaching methods that will help students from different linguistic and cultural backgrounds gain the background knowledge they need to access the social studies curriculum.

CURRICULA

The social studies curriculum is difficult for ELs for a number of reasons (Misco & Castañeda, 2009; de Oliveira, 2010). At the high school level, courses such as U.S. history and world history are traditionally taught sequentially, with the learning standards for each grade level scaffolding instruction from previous grades (Illinois States Board of Education, 2014). Depending on ELs' previous educational experiences, and their country of origin, there could be historical periods and contexts related to the content being taught in the U.S. classroom that are entirely new even for learners with strong prior schooling.

Textbooks used in history courses often use decontextualized language specific to this discipline and the level of instruction. Even timelines that may appear simple and not vocabulary laden may contain information that is not common knowledge to ELs from different cultural backgrounds. This challenge increases the reading comprehension load for learners who may also have limited experience reading expository text (Misco & Castañeda, 2009; de Oliveira, 2010). In this chapter the authors explore ways for teachers and ELs to overcome comprehension challenges in the social studies curriculum from elementary to secondary levels.

BEYOND ELEMENTARY SCHOOL

Students from middle school to high school experience different learning environments and face higher academic expectations from those required in elementary school (Haneda, 2009). From middle schooling levels on, the majority of school curricula are organized by classes focused on the individual disciplines, with each content area taught by teachers who may be credentialed only in one select discipline (Moje, 2008). This may result in less interdisciplinary collaboration across different departments, with potentially negative consequences for ELs.

ELs will benefit from the merging of instruction across content areas in interdisciplinary teaching formats that offer numerous opportunities to explore and use the same language in different contexts. This allows them to view a subject from different lenses and increases their active engagement in conversations that include exploring and developing conceptual knowledge plus the language needed be active participants in conversations.

History texts evolve from contextually laden narratives, which include visual support at the elementary level, to abstract expository presentations of events at the secondary level (Schleppegrell, 2004). A serious issue is that not all secondary mainstream teachers may understand that they must teach language, and that for ELs this involves addressing all language needed to gain students' comprehension of new ideas and interpretations. In order to access discipline-specific language and the concepts represented by historical terms, students need to understand and be able to use everyday language to make sense of new ideas and express these orally and in writing.

Further complicating the issue are students' attitudes towards social studies. Szpara and Ahmad (2007) documented that students consider social studies one of the least important courses in the curriculum. The dense language in historical texts can be incomprehensible for the student who does not have the funds of knowledge (González, 2005) to scaffold additional understandings. Teachers' perceptions of ELs' knowledge base is also a problem when students are mainstreamed based on criteria that does not include disciplinary specific language and concepts (Wolters & Pintrich, 1998). Teachers need to dedicate time to pre-evaluation in classrooms with ELs and to implement a well-planned anticipatory set in their lessons.

Teaching History Conceptually

History taught conceptually rather than sequentially helps all students comprehend. Erickson suggests that "through a conceptual lens, students are forced to analyze, evaluate, and investigate at deeper levels as they consider the transferable legitimacy of the data" (2008, p. 26). Probing for deeper understanding, she defines concepts as a "mental construct that is timeless, universal, and abstract (to different degrees)" (p. 30).

In the earlier years of the twentieth century, Harold Rugg (1936) cautioned against compartmentalizing history. He felt that in order to understand the complexities of society, knowledge should be "ramified ruthlessly across conventional subjects" (p. 336). Rugg believed that to prepare students to be democratic citizens requires that they participate in information getting, decision making, and community action.

ELs' Linguistic Diversity

History teachers often comment on the variety of language levels that ELs bring to their classrooms. These levels can range from speaking no English at all, to being proficient English speakers and all points in between. These authors believe that the best way to work with students at varying levels of language proficiency is to start teaching them where they are in their knowledge base. It serves no useful purpose to enumerate a long list of what the ELs cannot do. That attitude frustrates teachers and is a disservice to the students.

There is a resource that provides assistance to teachers both to identify ELs' language levels and to suggest ways to meet their language needs: the WIDA Can Do Descriptors (www.wida.us/standards/CAN_DOs). These descriptors provide goals for listening, speaking, reading, and writing for six progressive language levels. The WIDA descriptors help teachers identify the appropriate language function(s) needed to support ELs while they are learning historical content.

Delving into the Language of Social Studies

Gee (1992/2014) alerts us to keep in mind that the words ELs use acquire situated meanings through their experiences. Inside and outside of school there is a vast set of language needs facing ELs. They will use language as they work to understand and interpret message and as they come to fully grasp what is happening around them. At the same time, experiences allow them to access meaning and give shape to situated understanding of the context in which the learning is taking place. Teaching ELs vocabulary words without supporting context is as useful as asking that they read a book that is written in a language they do not know.

The key question that teachers ask is why the language used in the social studies classroom is difficult for ELs. Certainly, the concepts and the historical events that are the focus of the discipline are often unfamiliar to students from a different country. ELs' individual histories shape how they are able to access historical events in different contexts to understand, make sense of timelines, and ultimately judge what took place. ELs' experiences are also always unique to each learner. Teachers must be cautious as they plan instruction for culturally and linguistically diverse students because even when teaching all learners in English, their cultural capital may constitute the experiences of citizens residing in the Tower of Babel. Teachers must examine generalizations about ELs' cultural capital cautiously in evaluating how these can provide a clear lens of the learners' educational past and present needs.

Fang and Chapman (2015) help us understand that many difficulties relate to how historical texts are written from the lower to the higher grades. At the elementary school level, history is presented as "story-like representations of the past . . . where events are organized chronologically" (p. 3). In the upper grades, abstract interpretations of history tend to focus more on the *coverage model of history education* (Noonan, 2013; Sipress & Voelker, 2011). This model fails the ELs because its emphasis on breadth prevents their engagement in the type of argumentation that allows them to explore content as they use their entire language repertoire. We do not want the ELs to memorize facts without understanding their historical effects on our societies (Sipress & Voelker, 2011).

When the first author first arrived to the United States as a child, her past as a Cuban was delimited to the area where she had lived and traveled. She had not experienced slavery or the type of discrimination that was rampant in the United States in the early 1960s. She knew that in her country there were social clubs for different races but did not question the rationale for this separation of the races. She had not noted the discriminatory practices in her homeland. Perhaps because this type of segregation had been an accepted circumstance in Cuba, she did not relate it to what she saw in the United States upon arrival.

The topic of slavery had not been part of history courses in her country. After arrival to the United States, she selected to not take any history course until American history was required for graduation in the eleventh grade. In this course she struggled to understand the concept of slavery. The vocabulary used to present the content in the textbook and to discuss the topic in class added to challenges to comprehension.

She could not grasp the reason the Underground Railroad was mentioned in her history book because she was looking for railway cars and how these related to the topic that she was striving to understand: slavery. She did not know why someone might be labeled an Abolitionist nor did she know the word *abolish*. She could relate to the ideals of democracy because her family had fled the island of Cuba to escape communism. She had experienced dictatorships and communist regimes in which it was the norm to imprison those who disagreed with the political system and even kill them in the *paredón*/firing squad, but human slavery was an unfamiliar concept.

The confusion this learner experienced stemmed from not having the same sociocultural context as her classmates and from not being fluent in English. The teacher could have explicitly addressed the language of the content that she was teaching and the language necessary to discuss the topics but this was not the norm in this classroom. This would have helped the learner deconstruct the language of the text through close reading (Fang & Chapman, 2015). It is essential to help students examine the dense language of history texts so they do not waste instructional time focusing on a train that does not exist when studying the history of slavery in the United States.

Investigate Learners' Histories and Explore Background Knowledge

It is true that ELs come to the subject of U.S. history with a disadvantage of not experiencing the organic history of a unique country that develops on a daily basis. The same could be said of a U.S. citizen visiting a foreign country. There would be many historical signals that would be missed because of the day to day development of the history of a particular group of people. Simple political cartoons, laden with historical meaning, would go over most visitors' heads.

However, ELs have experienced evolving and often tumultuous histories in their own countries. They do have an extensive knowledge base of the history of their communities and countries. Those histories can be built upon when ELs examine and compare commonalities across their country of origin and past events in U.S. history.

There is a pattern in the formation of the identity of some countries. Compare the sequence of events in the formation of the United States and Mexico. In North America, Native peoples inhabited the land. Then when the Europeans came the spectrum of society changed. The rights of the indigenous inhabitants were frequently overlooked or blatantly denied by the Europeans.

The history books discuss how the settlers from across the ocean *conquered* a new world. The Europeans established settlements, agriculture, commerce, and trade that reflected their cultures of origin. Tensions developed between the motherland and the colonists, leading to a revolution. Eventually both the United States and Mexico gained freedom and were established as independent countries.

A history teacher could compare and contrast the formation of the United States with similar events in Mexico to help the ELs make connections with the U.S. history content. Even countries with a different pattern of identity formation as the U.S. demonstrate some type of sequence that led to their formation. That sequence could be used as a frame of reference for ELs regardless of their home country.

The example discussed previously of the EL arriving without a reference point to the concept of slavery in the United States or the discrimination of the 1960s could have been framed with a comparison of the slave trade in Cuba (Williams, 1970). This learner's knowledge base did not include a focus on slavery in her country in earlier centuries.

Cuba was dependent on slave trade from the 1780s to the 1860s. During that time the slave population in Cuba rose from 39,000 to 400,000. At the peak of the slave-based economy, the enslaved population in Cuba was one-third of the entire country's population. Slavery continued was in Cuba until 1886. While the curriculum in the 1960s in Cuba may not have discussed slavery in detail, there were likely references to it in the culture, if not in the history books, that could have helped the EL connect to the concept of slavery in the United States.

The point is that U.S. history was not created in isolation. Practically every county in the world played some part in the formation of the history of this nation. Clearly, the founding of the colonies was not done in isolation. England, France, Holland, Mexico, and Native American citizens in this continent all played a role in the formation and growth of the colonies. A multitude of countries participated in the slave trade, which provided the labor for the plantations of the south.

The ramifications of the U.S. Civil War reached Europe and beyond. Ronald Takaki (2008) summed up the complexity of U.S. history by saying that "you cannot spill a drop of American blood without spilling the blood of the whole world" (p. 20). Almost every EL who attends school in this nation can connect a part of his/her own country's history to that of the United States.

APPLICATIONS FOR THE CLASSROOM

Students will learn to wield any and all the language that their teachers include in their lessons and in classroom tasks, given the right support. Encourage ELs to be brave, to take chances, and to experiment using the new language they are learning as they demonstrate their evolving understandings, whether in listening, speaking, reading, or writing. Prepare them to do this by selecting appropriate texts to support content-area foci.

As ELs learn to deconstruct texts, they create new understandings when they take texts apart at the paragraph level and not at the single-word or sentence level. While in the process of taking students to use the new language subconsciously (without a dictionary or a glossary available), teachers must provide engaging and demanding classroom instruction while voicing high expectations for all students regardless of their level of English language proficiency.

One way to offer engaging multimodal instruction is through the use of graphic novels in history class. The graphic novel reduces the amount of text to the most important points. It allows ELs to visualize events in history. Graphic novels serve ELs well at the beginning stages of lessons that involve learning new language. As ELs develop higher English proficiencies, they will be moved into texts at higher language levels.

Lewis and Aydin (2013; 2015; 2016) recently released a three-volume graphic novel that would be very useful for ELs. It is a series called *The March*, chronicling the journey and fight for civil rights in the United States. Chun (2009) found that using the graphic novel *Maus* (Spiegelman, 2011) helped ELs understand the events of the Holocaust while in the process of developing English.

When selecting graphic novels for your classroom, ask yourself in what ways the novel is culturally appropriate for your student population and how it will allow the events covered in the history text to come alive for the ELs. Some reasons that graphic novels effectively support history lessons in classrooms with ELs are that:

- visuals give the students greater access to the message by scaffolding new information;
- short captions in the novels decrease the language load for the EL;
- narratives in the novels are less dense than expository history text so they will promote understanding of material covered in history class;

- text in these provides a narrative written in language more accessible for the EL to model;
- graphic novels supply comprehensible context and language for ELs to engage in critical analyses of text and dialogue with their peers and their teacher; and
- topics can offer opportunities to discuss important events in history that empower the ELs to know they have a voice in U.S. classrooms.

In conversations with students about the graphic novels you select for your classroom, ask them the same type of thoughtful questions that you would pose if they were reading any other type of narrative. Search for their voice and encourage them to express their ideas. Make a conscious effort to teach students to read with a critical literacy perspective. You might ask them some of the following questions (Daniel, 2016, p. 33):

- What is my opinion of the way the characters in this book act, dress, and speak to each other?
- How do I react to this topic?
- Is the way I think about this topic different from the author's?
- How would people in my culture react to this text?
- Do I understand why the author wrote this?
- What does this text tell me about the author?
- Is the author qualified to write this text?
- Do I detect any biased statements?
- Is the author privileging what is familiar to his/her culture group?
- What is the author not saying that I consider important?
- Are all voices heard in this author's words?
- Is there truth both in my interpretation and in the author's?

Functional Language Analysis

ELs are interested in language and in comparing and contrasting across their language repertoires. In their daily lives ELs engage in informal text analysis as part of making sense of their world. However, this may or may not yield them all the benefit possible in this process. Fang and Schleppegrell (2008) offer a procedure that teachers can use to engage students in purposeful and thoughtful reading across the content areas: functional language analysis (FLA). These steps address three key questions: what a text is about, how it is organized, and what the author's point of view is. Implementing this process requires the teacher:

1. select a short piece of a text that will be challenge the students' comprehension;

2. identify instructional goals: both in content and language;
3. identify the strategy that will be used and the metalanguage terms needed for the analysis; and
4. conduct the analysis "as a whole class, in small groups, or individually" (p. 111).

As students learn to conduct FLA, they answer key questions about the text, its organization, and the author's stance. Students identify main ideas and important details by looking at the clauses in the writing and the processes that are part of these. They identify the *verbs* used, the *participants*, their *attitudes and attributes*, and the *circumstances* (using adverbials and prepositional phrases). Students focus on the text's cohesion, on how clauses begin, and on *how clauses are combined* through *embedding*, *subordination*, or coordination.

The learners also investigate how the author sways the reader to develop a point of view. These authors consider this the most important question for ELs to explore because of the probability of high student engagement. The students "analyze each clause in terms of mood (i.e., declarative, interrogative, and imperative), modality (e.g., probability, obligation, seriousness), and word choices (e.g., nouns, verbs, adjectives)" (Fang & Chapman, 2015, p. 11).

Learning History through Art

The images in art provide strong representations of historical events. Viewing images of certain historical events also provides needed contextual support for ELs. For example, the study of the Great Migration, the movement of African Americans who left their homes in the south to travel to the north for better working conditions, can be introduced through the artwork of Jacob Lawrence (1993; 2016). A linking language strategy (Herrera, 2016) could be used to introduce the topic.

Linking language allows teachers to learn about students' background knowledge. To begin the activity, a teacher chooses eight examples from the art of Lawrence depicting the Great Migration that illustrate the key ideas of the event. Each art sample is attached to one large sheet of chart paper. These are displayed on a student table or taped to the classroom wall. Then in groups of four to five, students walk from paper to paper, writing or drawing everything they think or feel when they look at the picture.

During the process of exploring history through art, students are encouraged to use the language of their choice. At the end of the anticipatory conversation, the teacher circles any key words that relate to the target vocabulary of the day. Once the students' vocabulary and prior knowledge of the Great Migration has been brought forward, the teacher begins the lesson.

A next step might be to read the book *The Great Migration: An American Story* by Jacob Lawrence. Learning activities can be found at www.phillipscollection.org/research/american_art/learning/lawrence-migration_learning1.htm.

The topic of children in the civil rights movement can also be introduced using Norman Rockwell's painting *The Problem We All Live With*. Rockwell depicted the integration of the William Franz Elementary school in Louisiana in 1960 by first-grader Ruby Bridges. In her time as an elementary-level teacher, this chapter's second author would begin this lesson by showing Rockwell's painting of the event.

Interestingly, she found that very few of her students were aware of this particular event, not just the ELs. Thus, it appears that the background knowledge among the students in a lesson that included this painting is often on a level playing field. The painting graphically depicts the event showing four U.S. Marshals walking Ruby Bridges to school. A red tomato has been thrown and smashed against the wall. The N word is very prominent as are the letters KKK for the Ku Klux Clan.

This painting evokes emotions from every student that views it, which taps into what Herrera (2016) calls the sociocultural dimension. This means the teacher must encourage the learners to utilize their prior knowledge and understandings of the world to interpret the ideas in the painting. The potential for student sharing of their perspectives in this activity enriches everyone in the classroom, including the teacher.

Taking Action: Collaborative Discussions

Despite the many challenges facing ELs in the social studies classroom, teachers can provide instruction that promotes a high level of literacy and language development for all students. Educators can collaborate to make the secondary social studies curriculum relevant for both ELs and general education students.

At this point, the chapter's third author will identify select historical events that may pose an interesting challenge in planning lessons for ELs. She then offers a rationale for designing lessons and effective strategies for teaching and learning. You will see why the *coverage model* of history education fails to educate ELs and that indeed teachers can reach the students effectively in many other ways.

The Secondary Curriculum

As noted previously, one of the challenges facing ELs in the secondary social studies classroom is the amount of content taught in the traditional curriculum. After several years of struggling to engage high school students excited about U.S. history, the members of a history department worked to revamp the existing curriculum. With the support of the school principal, the group piloted a curriculum focused on covering fewer topics and doing so within a thematic framework.

When choosing the themes for the course, the social studies department faculty started with the student population in mind. In addition to identifying topics in which students showed an interest, the teachers also wanted the curriculum to be indicative of the issues and problems that the United States has faced in the past and continues to face. Each teacher made a top-ten list of possible topics using these two criteria. After much discussion, the list was narrowed down to include topics such as immigration, war and foreign policy, the government's role in society, and the struggle for social equality. These topics each became a unit of study for the course. Whereas before the curriculum consisted of fourteen units of study within the yearlong course, now the teachers would focus in-depth on only seven units.

In addition to limiting the number of instructional units, each unit was centered on an essential question. The essential question was used to frame the content that would be taught in the unit. Only content that was necessary to answering the essential question was included in the unit of instruction. For example, the essential question *When is war justified?* was used to frame the unit on war and foreign policy.

Traditional memorization of specific battles, dates, and casualties was replaced by analyzing the reasons the United States has entered into different wars in history and the impacts associated with these wars. For ELs, the essential question is instrumental in helping them *anchor* the unit content to a common purpose. Rather than seeing history as a myriad of unconnected facts and events, the essential question provided the glue to help students make connections.

As the teachers planned each unit of study, they wanted to keep the relevance of each theme in the forefront. They planned to begin each unit by studying a current issue related to the theme. The goal was to *hook* the students with an issue they were hearing about in the news and begin the unit with something about which students had some background knowledge. Once hooked on the topic, the unit would take students back in time to different episodes in history and trace the issue up to its current status.

This method uses the study of the past to explain why things are the way they are today. By using this approach, ELs are able to start with their own background knowledge and build from it. Starting with a current issue also allows teachers to pre-assess students' initial understanding of the concept.

While not all teachers have the latitude to experiment and pilot a new curriculum, there are things teachers do have control over as they plan curricular units. Despite teaching in a traditional, chronological approach, teachers can ask themselves, *What is the big picture of this unit? What is the theme of this unit that I want my students to walk away with?* In determining this *big picture idea*, teachers can tie it to something current. Teachers also control the essential questions that anchor the units. Again, using the *big picture idea*, try to frame a question that encompasses the idea and the content that students would need to know in order to answer the question. By keeping these ideas at the forefront while planning instruction, you will also be helping ELs overcome the challenge of content overload.

An appropriate unit for classrooms with ELs is titled *The Quest for Equality*. The essential question for this unit is, *To what extent have marginalized groups achieved equality in the United States?* There are many current events that could be used to hook students, one being the Black Lives Matter movement or the Dakota Access Pipeline's impact on Native American tribes. ELs are often drawn to this particular unit because many of them have a personal connection to the topic of discrimination. The next section will explore a specific lesson used in the study of this unit.

Planning a Lesson on Equality

The introductory lesson to hook students into this unit starts with an overview of current equality issues in the United States. Students are presented with a spectrum that reads, *full equality* on one end and *no equality* on the other end. Students are asked to rate where they perceive various minorities, including women, indigenous Americans, African Americans, and Latino Americans, fall on this spectrum. Students discuss in pairs where they placed the different minority groups. A brief whole-class discussion occurs in which students share some commonalities they found with their partner. This lesson takes students to look beyond their immediate surroundings. Many students share the misconception that life is well for all minority groups because what the standard curriculum presents to them is that these groups are fully equal in U.S. society.

Next, students are given a list of statistics and asked to determine if the statement is a true or false statistic. The teacher involves the learners in a conversation centered on what makes a statistic valid versus invalid. The statistics shared include differences in men and women's salaries, graduation rates of Native Americans, and incarceration rates of African American males. Most of the statistics are true, which surprises many students and creates a cognitive dissonance to their initial perceptions.

Whole-class discussion ensues about why the statistics are a surprise to the students. They share ideas about what might account for the disparities between racial and ethnic minorities and whites. This discussion brings up the concept of equal rights versus equal opportunities. Students struggle with the idea that the achievement of equal rights does not guarantee equality when there are still differences in wealth, education, and power. This is *the hook* that engages students into the unit, especially ELs who at times have experienced these aspects in their own lives.

Once students' interest is captured, the unit proceeds by taking the learners back in time to explore the various types of discrimination that occurred in the nation in different eras. By approaching these events in a thematic way, students are better able to compare the experiences of different groups discriminated against and the actions they took to achieve equal rights. In order to answer the essential question of to what extent minority groups have achieved equality in the United States, students have to understand the struggles that these groups have encountered, the actions group members took to create change, and the successes that have been achieved.

CONCLUSIONS AND RECOMMENDATIONS FOR THE CLASSROOM

Remember that as a teacher you are not alone in your work. One common obstacle teachers seem to face is not having enough time to do what they feel they need to do. There are solutions to the time crunch if teachers, staff, students, and parents work together. The African saying "It takes a village to raise a child" is true for schools too.

1. *Join with the art teacher to help your ELs understand historical events*. Selecting artwork does take time, but if you ask the art teacher to help, that search might be done in a matter of minutes. The art teacher may already be familiar with art that would fit into your instructional topic. The key to utilizing the faculty and staff is in knowing where the expertise lies. For example, a high school history teacher began a project about the Sudan based on an interaction he had with a custodian. The custodian was a college student who asked the teacher where the meeting was focused on the Sudan. The college student had heard about the genocide and wanted to offer help. One thing led to another and the history teacher ended up making a full-length documentary and unit for his students about the genocide in the region of the Sudan. The background for the development of this documentary can be found at www.socialstudies.com/pdf/BBC102DVG.pdf.
2. *Let the experts enter into your space*. Author 2 was invited to a session with a reading teacher who was sharing ideas to help struggling ELs. All the primary-grade teachers were invited but only the kindergarten teacher and author 2 participated. She learned new things. No one person has all the knowledge! We all can learn from others!
3. *Observe your students*. Another common concern among teachers is learning about the backgrounds and language levels of ELs. Teachers

first think about testing all the students to learn about language levels. I am reminded of a new teacher who asked for a test that could measure a student's language ability. She was tutoring the student. I suggested that she had enough background knowledge about language development at that age that she could have a conversation with the student and determine his language level herself; in this case she did not need a test. While testing is one way to learn about students, there is another possibly more practical solution. Teachers can use their powers of observation combined with their experience and pedagogical knowledge. Too many times teachers think that the only way to learn about students is through tests, but it is time that teachers start trusting themselves and their amazing knowledge base.

Stop and watch a group of students for ten to fifteen minutes. Then write down all that you learned about them. Don't hold back. Any piece of information could be useful. Finally, compare your list to what you might learn about those same students from a test. It is true that tests have their place but they are not the only way a teacher can get information. I predict that you will find that you have learned a great deal of useful information about the students through your own observations and talking with and listening to students throughout the day.

4. *Welcome the parents to help you.* Family members can provide a great deal of information about students' cultural background. Prepare a survey for parents asking for background information about the children. It is true that not all parents will send these surveys back but the information from those that *are* returned can be useful. Call parents who do not return the survey and ask them to share what they view as their child's strengths. The key to eliciting parental cooperation is to show that you are on the side of the child and that the parents will be helping you to better plan instruction. There will be time later for phone calls about behavior and learning issues. Remember that *it takes two positive statements* to stay even with one negative statement. Another point to remember when contacting parents is the old adage that you catch more flies with honey than with vinegar.

5. *Reach out to parents.* Go to where the parents are. One school district offered workshops to parents who came to the food pantry early. School administrators realized that parents were lining up one hour early and standing in the cold just to be on time for when the pantry opened. They invited the parents into the multipurpose room and offered workshops. The parents were very appreciative because they wanted to learn how to help their children. It was a win-win solution for all involved. Every teacher's situation will be different, but think

about ways that you could reach out to parents that would make it easy for them to share information.

RESOURCES AND RECOMMENDATIONS FOR TEACHERS

Background knowledge for the Great Migration can be found at:

- www.history.com/topics/black-history/great-migration.
- Lawrence, J. (2016) The Great Migration. Retrieved from www.phillipscollection.org/research/american_art/artwork/Lawrence-Migration_Series1.htm and www.phillipscollection.org/migration_series.
- Learning activities for the Great Migration retrieved on September 3, 2016, from www.phillipscollection.org/research/american_art/learning/lawrence-migration_learning1.htm.
- A study of Norman Rockwell written by the former director of the Brooklyn Museum. Includes reproductions of six hundred of Rockwell's best illustrations and provides a panorama of nearly sixty years of American social history.
- Buechner, T. S. (1972). *Norman Rockwell, A sixty-year retrospective*. New York, NY: H. Abrams.
- Norman Rockwell Museum website. Includes images, information, teacher resources, and a family guide: www.nrm.org.
- This website highlights an episode of National Public Radio's *The Picture Show* focusing on the exhibition Norman Rockwell: Behind the Camera. Includes photo gallery and interactives such as Weekend Edition Sunday story by NPR's Jacki Lyden. www.pbs.org/wnet/aaworld/history/spotlight_september.html and www.npr.org/blogs/pictureshow/2009/11/rockwell.html.

Text resources about Ruby Bridges:

- Bridges's memoir is presented from her own perspective as a six-year-old. Appropriate for readers nine to twelve years old. Bridges, R. (1999). *Through My Eyes*. New York, NY: Scholastic Press.
- This book tells the story of Ruby Bridges's first year of school through words and watercolor illustrations. Coles, R. (1995). *The Story of Ruby Bridges*. New York, NY: Scholastic Press.

Web-based resources on Ruby Bridges:

- The official website of Ruby Bridges. Includes information on the Ruby Bridges Foundation, which she formed in 1999 to promote "the values of

tolerance, respect, and appreciation of all differences." www.rubybridges.com/home.htm.
- African American World: The PBS Guide to African American History and Culture. Includes excerpts from Ruby Bridges's autobiography.
- The Anti-Defamation League's lessons for teaching about Brown vs. Board of Education. www.adl.org/education/brown_2004/default.asp.
- Short interviews with Ruby Bridges: www.watchknowlearn.org/Video.aspx?VideoID=41899&CategoryID=1051; www.youtube.com/watch?v=ecBORXfap9A Interview; www.youtube.com/watch?v=Ur5iF-qp8-8 Life and Times of Ruby Bridges.

REFERENCES

Chun, C. (2009). Critical literacies and graphic novels for English-language learners: Teaching *Maus*. *Journal of Adolescent and Adult Literacy, 53*(2), 144–153. doi:10.1598/JAAL.53.2.5

Daniel, M. (2016). Critical pedagogy's power in English language teaching. In L. R. Jacobs & C. Hastings (Eds.), *The importance of social justice in English language teaching* (pp. 25–38). Alexandria, VA: TESOL Press.

de Oliveira, L. (2010). Nouns in history: Packaging information, expanding explanations, and structuring reasoning. *The History Teacher, 43*(2), 191–203.

Erickson, H. L. (2008). *Stirring the head, heart, and soul: Redefining curriculum, instruction, and concept-based teaching.* Thousand Oaks, CA: Corwin Press

Fang, Z., & Chapman, Z. (2015). Enhancing English learners' access to disciplinary texts through close reading practices. In M. Daniel & K. Mokhtari (Eds.), *Research-based instruction that makes a difference in English learners' success* (pp. 3–17). Lanham, MD: Rowman and Littlefield.

Fang, Z., & Schleppegrell, M. J. (2008). *Reading in secondary content areas: A language-based pedagogy.* Ann Arbor, MI: University of Michigan.

Gee, J. (1992/2014). *The social mind.* Champaign-Urbana, IL: Common Ground.

González, N. (2005). Beyond culture: The hybridity of funds of knowledge. In N. González, L. C. Moll, & C. Amanti (Eds.), *Funds of knowledge: Theorizing practices in households, communities, and classrooms* (pp. 29–46). New York, NY: Routledge.

Haneda, M. (2009). Learning about the past and preparing for the future: A longitudinal investigation of a grade 7 'sheltered' social studies class. *Language and Education, 23*(4), 335–352.

Illinois State Board of Education (ISBE). (2014). *Illinois learning standards: Social science.* Retrieved from www.isbe.net/ils/social_science/standards.htm.

Lawrence, J. (1993). *The great migration: An American story.* New York, NY: The Museum of Modern Art.

Lewis, J., & Aydin, A. (2013). *The march: Book one.* Marietta, GA: Top Shelf Productions.

Lewis, J., & Aydin, A. (2015). *The march: Book two.* Marietta, GA: Top Shelf Productions.

Lewis, J., & Aydin, A. (2016). *The march: Book three.* Marietta, GA: Top Shelf Productions.

Misco, T., & Castañeda, M. (2009). "Now, what should I do for English language learners?" Reconceptualizing social studies curriculum design for ELLs. *Educational Horizons, 87*(3), 183–189.

Moje, E. (2008). Foregrounding the disciplines in secondary literacy teaching and learning: A call for change. *Journal of Adolescent and Adult Literacy, 52*(2), 96–107.

Noonan, E. (2013). The history textbook, born digital. *Radical History Review, 117*, 131–138. doi: 10.1215/01636545-2210658

Rugg, H. (1936). *American life and the school curriculum: Next steps towards schools of living.* Boston, MA: Ginn and Co.

Schleppegrell, M. (2004). *The language of schooling: A functional linguistics perspective.* Mahwah, NJ: Lawrence Erlbaum Associates.

Sipress, J., & Voelker, D. (2011). The end of the history survey course: The rise and fall of the coverage model. *The Journal of American History, 97*(4), 1050–1066.

Spiegelman, A. (2011). *Maus: A survivor's tale.* New York, NY: Pantheon Books.

Szpara, M., & Ahmad, I. (2007). Supporting English-language learners in social studies class: Results from a study of high school teachers. *The Social Studies, 98*(5), 189–196.

Takaki, R. (2008). *A different mirror: A history of multicultural America.* New York, NY: Back Bay Books, Little, Brown.

WIDA Can Do Descriptors. Retrieved from www.wida.us/standards/CAN_DO

Williams, E. (1970). *From Columbus to Castro: A history of the Caribbean, 1492-1969.* New York, NY: Vintage Books.

Wolters, C., & Pintrich, P. (1998). Contextual differences in student motivation and self-regulated learning in mathematics, English, and social studies classrooms. *Instructional Science, 26*(1–2), 27–47.

III

Evaluation for Learning

Chapter Seven

Assessing English Learner Readers at Levels K–12

Kathrine Crane Rockwell and Rona F. Flippo

Teachers hold the cards when evaluating English learners. Their actions ensure assessments for English learners are equitable. They improve the process by differentiating existing evaluations, interpreting data effectively, using strategy and schema assessments, and supporting English learners who take high-stakes standardized tests.

Schools today must be ready to serve more language-diverse youngsters than ever before. However, many teachers feel unprepared and/or unequipped to provide quality assessment and instruction for English language learners (ELs). Unfortunately, many teachers report that they have received inadequate professional training or do not have access to appropriate resources, tools, and materials to teach ELs successfully (Gandara et al., 2005). Teachers want to learn how to assess these students, so with teachers' guidance and support, the students will be able to succeed in their content studies as well as in their language acquisition and development of reading, writing, study, and related literacy skills.

ELs are a diverse subgroup of students. In a single school, teachers may work with ELs who have recently immigrated, as well as those who have lived in the United States since birth. Some EL students come from homes where no English is spoken, while others come from homes where English is spoken alongside another language. Home language(s), cultural norms, home literacy habits, religious practices, socioeconomic factors, and beliefs about education may vary among the EL populations that are in today's classrooms. There is no one-size-fits-all approach to differentiating instruction or assessment for ELs.

It is not possible to make generalizations about learning and assessment among this student group because of several factors. What may be true about newcomer ELs from one background may not be true of ELs who were born and grew up in the United States. EL enrollments are unstable, because students exit the EL subgroup once they have met criteria for English proficiency.

Assessment protocols and student population change year to year (the same student does not take the same assessment over and over again; annual versions of a state reading assessment could be linguistically different from one another). Lastly, the definition of who is considered an EL may vary from state to state, depending on how criteria for inclusion in the subgroup are interpreted (Abedi & Gandara, 2006). Such dynamic circumstances make it challenging to measure trends among these populations. However, researchers have found that the following information merits consideration:

- ELs tend to score lower than non-ELs on large-scale summative tests, such as the NAEP, and high-stakes state-mandated tests that are tied to federal funding programs (U.S. Department of Education, 2010–2014; Abedi & Levine, 2013).
- Children tend to have more successful reading experiences when some aspect of the text reflects their own understanding of the world. Personal and cultural relevance, and interest of text topics, may affect reading comprehension, engagement, and the appropriateness of miscues (Au, 1998; Compton-Lilly, 2006; Flippo, 2014; Freeman & Freeman, 2007; Gambrell, 2015; Goodman, 1982; Risko & Walker-Dalhouse, 2007).
- Assessment of ELs' learning is most accurate and appropriate when multiple measures are used, including alternative assessments, and considered alongside a thorough knowledge of the student and his or her cultural, linguistic, and educational background (Lenski et al., 2006; Fountas & Pinnell, 2001; Rothenberg & Fisher, 2007).
- ELs' language development may prevent them from demonstrating proficiency with content-area skills on some assessments, which impacts the content validity (the extent to which a test accurately measures what it was designed to measure) of the assessment (Heubert & Hauser, 1999).
- Alternative, informal, and formative assessments can and should be used when possible and appropriate (Lenski et al., 2006; Echevarria et al., 2008; Fountas & Pinnell, 2001).
- Typically, students develop basic social language first, and more complex, specific, and academic language later. Cummins (1979) refers to developing this second type of language as Cognitive Academic Language Proficiency (CALP), and finds that it takes significantly longer than social language to develop (Cummins, 1984).

- High-stakes tests and standards-based curricula involve increasingly complex language demands (Hakuta, 2014).

PRACTICAL APPLICATIONS

For every challenge involved in EL assessment, there is an opportunity for teachers to improve the process. Teachers can help students to become familiar with the academic language seen on standardized tests, and model strategies to use when encountering difficult texts. Data from summative, diagnostic, and standardized tests can be considered carefully with a student's developing English skills in mind. Teacher-created assessments can be differentiated to make them more accessible and comprehensible to ELs. The following suggestions will help teachers collect and interpret valuable data about EL learning and make the assessment process worthwhile for all involved.

Literacy Assessments: Read-and-Retell

Many teachers will administer periodic reading assessments that involve a running record and a retelling component. The exact procedure for these varies and they can serve several purposes. Teachers trained in literacy diagnosis and assessment may administer these assessments in order to perform miscue analysis. This qualitative examination of data can inform instruction and help teachers make decisions about grouping students, text selection, and instructional pacing.

By contrast, many school districts now require periodic assessment of student reading progress (sometimes referred to as progress monitoring or benchmarking). Assessments that are currently used for this purpose include the Developmental Reading Assessment (DRA) (Beaver, 2002) and Fountas and Pinnell Benchmark Assessment Systems 1 & 2 (Fountas, 2008; Fountas & Pinnell, 2007). These assessments are commercially prepared kits that are provided to teachers by school districts for the purpose of evaluating students' reading progress.

When these literacy assessments are performed with ELs, teachers should consider how cultural bias in texts might impact student understanding. A casual survey of texts used in an elementary assessment kit reveals stories that depict what might be described as typical of life in the United States—such as going to sleepovers. For the majority of English-speaking children born in the United States, these topics and settings may be familiar and easy to understand. Some ELs, however, may have difficulty recognizing the cultural institutions depicted in these books. In turn it may be difficult for them to make inferences and use their prior knowledge to understand the story.

> Analiese read a book about taking the dog to the groomer. People would not typically take a dog to the groomer where she is from. In her student's retelling, she discusses how the dog was brought to the doctor—a conclusion that she drew based on the illustrations of a dog and a man in a white coat.

If teachers believe that students do not have enough background knowledge to fully comprehend a text, they may want to conduct a picture walk that asks the learners to talk about the title of the book. Then have students read the book jacket or back cover. Teachers may also present background information about the setting/topic prior to beginning to read. Teachers may want to retest students with a different text at the same reading level if teachers believe that a lack of cultural familiarity has negatively impacted the students' understanding.

Pronunciation and fluency also cause problems for some ELs. In some languages, not all letters that appear in print are pronounced when reading out loud. ELs may slow their rate of reading or change their intonation. In other languages, the sounds made by letters vary from those heard in English. Phonics patterns and rules may apply differently in an EL's home language(s). ELs who are literate in two or more languages may understand a single letter to have multiple possibilities of letter-sound correspondence. For example, the letter *y* predominantly produces an ē sound in French (as in "Yves"). A student who is literate in French may transfer that knowledge when pronouncing English words that pronounce *y* as an ī (the word *pry* might be pronounced *pree*). This does not represent a misunderstanding of the sound that the letter makes, but shows that the student has an extended understanding of how the letter is used across two languages.

> Marcel reads from a book in his school's literacy assessment kit. During the assessment, his teacher notes that he does not say the "s" out loud at the end of words such as "dogs" and "drums." This brings Marcel's score down, and he scores much lower than matches his comprehension. His teacher, Mrs. Rodriguez, is concerned. During his retelling, it is obvious that Marcel has comprehended the text well and, despite the errors in pronouncing plural nouns, he reads fluently, efficiently, and with proper intonation.

Some commercial assessments caution teachers against identifying these pronunciation challenges as miscues. The goal of such an accommodation is not to make assessments easier or more forgiving for ELs, but to account for a normal phase in the development of reading in a developing language.

At other times, teachers may be instructed or taught to count variations in pronunciation as "errors." While teachers must follow school district guidelines for the purposes of score reporting and data collection, they should use their judgment when they analyze and apply data for instructional purposes (Flippo et al., 2009).

Syntax may also cause problems for students taking select literacy progress assessments. Students may be unfamiliar with the structure of texts used during these exercises. Students who are used to hearing and reading a language other than English may not notice deviations from standard English syntax (they may not detect /hear when a phrase or a sentence is not correct) because these students do not have the second language mastery to do so.

> Virgella entered U.S. schools part way through the previous academic year. When speaking, she sometimes has trouble with subject and object pronouns. During her literacy assessment, she frequently replaces the personal pronoun he with the object pronoun him, and she with her, as she does when speaking. Although she has made progress in her reading, this repeated miscue brings down her scores, and, as a consequence, her recommended reading level.
>
> Her classroom teacher, the school reading teacher, and the ESL teacher discuss the assessment. They decide to provide targeted instruction and practice with pronouns, both in oral activities and in reading. They reassess her again after three weeks of the targeted instruction. While Virgella still occasionally makes errors with pronouns, it happens less frequently, and her score and reading level are now adjusted.

Hopefully, teachers do not use the reading level determined by one single assessment as the sole basis for grouping, skill instruction, and text selection for a student. In fact, while the information from these assessments may seem expedient or even helpful, teachers should use multiple assessments and measures of reading to group students and make instructional decisions (Lenski et al., 2006; Fountas & Pinnell, 2001; Echevarria et al., 2008), such as the strategy-based groupings described in Flippo (2014).

ASSESSING EMERGING EL READERS IN CONTENT-AREA CLASSROOMS

Teachers of English, language arts, writing, and reading are not the only educators who assess students' reading progress and strategy use, but the degree to which language is involved in all areas of teaching and learning is often underappreciated. In the upper grades, for example, biology or algebra teachers may not view themselves as reading or writing teachers. Of course, the four domains of English language (speaking, listening, reading, and writing) are used in content classrooms daily, where the complex structure of subject-area texts requires a specific set of reading skills. Therefore, content teachers are indeed teachers of the reading and writing (as well as speaking and listening) that is related to the subject(s) that they teach. These teachers need to think carefully about the assessments that they use and modify them to be compatible with their ELs' language proficiency level. It may also help these teachers to develop metacognitive, strategy, and schematic assessments to help them better evaluate students and to adjust their instruction accordingly. Of course, this does not mean that teachers must reinvent the wheel and create individual assessments for each of their students.

> Mr. Murray has been teaching his fourth-grade students about the rock cycle. They have read texts and watched videos that described how rocks change over millennia. In groups, they created models of igneous, metamorphic, and sedimentary rocks. Three of his students are developing ELs (they have been exposed to and learning English for less than three years), and two of his students are newcomers who come to his class for science only.
>
> Mr. Murray wants to reuse his assessment from years past, but wonders if the test (which involves a labeling activity, multiple-choice questions, and a cloze passage) will accurately assess what his ELs have learned. After discussing the assessment with the ESL specialist in his building, he adjusts the assessment for his ELs.
>
> All students participate in the labeling activity. A word bank is created for all students to use. A teacher sits with the newcomer students and reads the directions and questions aloud. (As part of this modification, the teacher also paraphrases and answers questions.) The ESL specialist assists Mr. Murray in modifying the multiple choice and cloze items. She simplifies the language that Mr. Murray used, yet keeps the gist of the questions the same. She also adds pictures and symbols to the multiple-choice options to provide students graphic support as they answer questions.
>
> Rather than complete the cloze and multiple-choice components of the test, newcomer students give an oral explanation of the rock cycle, which a teacher records and scores with a rubric. The students are given realia and picture cards to assist them with their explanation.

Significant thought, and a fair amount of time, was put into the adjustments made to Mr. Murray's assessment. Consulting and collaborating with his school's ESL specialist resulted in a better assessment.

STRATEGY AND SCHEMA ASSESSMENTS

The importance of schema in meaning making has been well-documented and known for decades (Carrell, 1984; Pearson et al., 1979). Students comprehend more when they have sufficient contextual knowledge. Teachers of ELs should be particularly sensitive to the role background knowledge plays in reading comprehension, as ELs may be more likely to be disadvantaged by the cultural bias present in reading selections. Teachers can informally probe students' prior knowledge, and activate existing knowledge, by conducting appropriate pre-reading activities and engaging in dialogue with students. Picture walks or discussions where the teacher asks students to "tell me what you know about . . ." are very effective. Prior to reading Beverly Cleary's *The Mouse and the Motorcycle,* teachers and students can discuss what it might be like to be very small. Before sharing Tomie DePaola's *Strega Nona*, teachers can show a picture of a recent spaghetti dinner and talk about magic spells. More comprehensive assessments of schema could include having students respond to a journal prompt or complete a KWL chart.

In addition to modifying content-area assessments, teachers in the upper grades can also learn a great deal about ELs by administering both strategy and schema assessments. Flippo (2014) provides many examples of strategy and schema assessments that can be easily administered in the mainstream classroom. Data from these assessments may be particularly helpful when ELs *seem* to be proficient in the four domains of language, but do not fully comprehend assigned content-area readings.

> At a departmental meeting, Mr. Murray is speaking with other science teachers in his district about assessing ELs in the mainstream classroom. A middle-school colleague talks about how she assessed students' strategy use.
>
> "I have been allowing my students to use their class notes on my in-class tests. I felt that this would help some of my struggling students, and in particular a few of my ELs. This didn't work out as well as I had hoped though, and when I spoke with our ESL specialist, she mentioned that the students might not have developed strong note-taking strategies. So we worked together to assess that particular skill.
>
> "We created note-taking scavenger hunt, where students had to take notes of chunks of text, looking for clues. We specified on the annotated notes paper the page numbers where the first bits of information could be found.
>
> "When we looked at the notes that the students brought back, we were able to see that some of them were not sure how to organize their information. We also saw that some students prioritized smaller facts and data over big ideas in the text. Finally, we noticed that students were not using the information contained in pictures and diagrams as part of their note taking. The ESL specialist used this information as a basis for enrichment activities in his own classroom, and I continued to model note-taking sections of the text."

EXAMINING THE LANGUAGE USED IN EVALUATIONS

As stressed previously in this chapter, making classroom assessments more accessible to ELs depends on the assessment, the objectives of what you have taught, and most importantly, the students themselves. Inspired by previous work on assessment (Flippo et al., 2015), here are a few more ideas applicable to specific types of assessments that teachers may want to try:

Multiple Choice Questions

Inventory the multiple-choice questions that you are currently using (for both teacher-made tests and other classroom-based activities that are used as assessments), and examine the language used on these assessments. Decide whether the questions are being asked in the most direct way possible. Eliminate language that is unnecessary to the scope of the assessment.

> After the success of the rock cycle assessment, Mr. Murray begins to plan an upcoming unit assessment for his next unit, which covers the phases of the moon. He reads over the multiple-choice items that he has used in years past and modifies questions to make the language as clear and direct as possible. He also modifies the answer selections so that they restate the question, use fewer pronouns (which can be abstract or vague), and more closely follow how he verbally makes points of emphasis in his classroom. Here is an example:
> *(Original multiple-choice question)*
> Why is the moon visible to people on earth?
>
> a. It is hot.
> b. It is frozen.
> c. There are volcanoes on its surface.
> d. The light of the sun shines on it and can be seen on earth.
>
> *(Revised multiple choice question)*
> Why do we see the moon from earth?
>
> a. We see the moon because it is hot.
> b. We see the moon because it is frozen.
> c. We see the moon because it has volcanoes.
> d. We see the moon because the sun's light shines on it.
>
> The revised question refers to clear subjects and objects (*we, the moon*), and the sentences follow a familiar pattern (effect-because-cause).

Abedi and Linquanti (2012) present examples of what they refer to as "language difficulties" that may impact test outcomes: "unfamiliar vocabulary, complex grammatical structures, nominalization, multiple embedded clauses, and passive voice constructions" (p. 4). They also analyze the language used on a released-item math word problem, noting that changes can be made in the problem with regards to word choice, technically accurate vocabulary (bakery vs. cookie factory), use of modal verbs, and use of subordinate clauses. If a class has a significant EL population, consider reading questions aloud before having students begin the test and paraphrasing more complex language. (For classrooms with only a few EL students, consider having them take the test with their ESL faculty member, or in a smaller group, where you can read aloud and paraphrase as needed.)

Essay Questions

For an EL, a single essay question, assigned in a content area, could be the product of an entire year's worth of learning and application. Explaining how photosynthesis occurs, for example, requires thorough understanding of the content topic. In order to write clearly and accurately about the topic, a student would need to use specific, technical vocabulary, such as *chlorophyll*, *energy*, and *respiration*. The student would also need to use academic language that is specific to a sequence of events, describing a scientific process, and cause and effect. Finally, the EL would have to have enough knowledge of standard English conventions to produce writing that can be read and understood. Because successful essay questions require the knowledge of content vocabulary, academic language, and grammar as detailed above, teachers should provide ELs with as much support as possible if they use essay questions as a part of their assessment repertoire. Some helpful supports might include sentence starters, graphic organizers, word banks, and informational tools such as diagrams or timelines. Here is an example from a U.S. history assessment:

(Original version)
"Discuss how the French involvement in the American Revolution was critical to the success of the colonial army. Cite specific examples in your essay."

Note that this question does not explicitly tell the student to write an essay—it is assumed by mentioning an essay in the second sentence that the student understands this expectation.

(Revised version)
"How did the French military help Washington's Army win the Revolutionary War? Write an essay to answer this question."

The revised prompt clearly states what the student is supposed to do (write an essay), and the topic of the essay is stated more directly, in the form of a question. Additional support for this question may also include a sentence starter, a timeline of events, an annotated graphic organizer (showing where to include specific examples), and a word bank containing transition words and key content vocabulary (*Washington*, *colonial*, *navy*).

These supports reduce the overall language demand that is placed on the students, allowing them to focus on writing an essay that shows their understanding of French involvement in the American Revolution—likely resulting in a more valid U.S. history assessment.

In the examples presented, reducing the amount of vague, abstract, or flowery academic language produces assessments that are more compatible with a wider range of students' English proficiency. While teaching, modeling, and promoting the use of academic language is vitally important, we want to ensure that complex language on an assessment will not skew results. Students cannot be determined to fail science tests or not meet civics objectives that, if not for the language used on the assessment, they would have otherwise met. Evaluation should serve to help students build confidence with using the English language across all four domains.

CONCLUSIONS AND RECOMMENDATIONS FOR ACTION

1. *Seek Student Feedback about Assessment:* You may feel that you know your students well, but ask yourself if you fully understand how the ELs feel about school. While it is possible to gauge students' feelings and attitudes as they relate to testing and assessments, there may be pieces of the puzzle that merit further investigation. To help you have a more accurate picture of how students feel about assessment and how they perceive their own learning, engage them in unstructured discussions after evaluations, ask them to complete anonymous surveys about assessment attitudes and concerns, and ask them to write post-assessment reflections. What follows are some examples of questions that you might consider using:

- What is one piece of work that you have done at school that makes you very proud? Why does that piece of work make you proud?
- Which activity in our class do you enjoy the least?
- How do you feel about taking a spelling test each week?
- What strategies do you use when you come to a difficult question on a test or quiz?
- Which of these tools are helpful to you on a test: word banks, sentence starters, pictures, word wall, receiving help from your teacher?
- Do you get upset if you cannot finish a test or quiz in time?
- Do you think that tests are more difficult if they have a time limit?
- Do you know what you should do when a teacher tells you to "check your work"?
- When a teacher gives you a project to do at home, is someone at home able to help you?

2. *Create Face-to-Face Time with the ESL Specialist.* As illustrated by the examples in this chapter, ESL faculty may be able to model teaching strategies, differentiate assessments, and provide insight about ELs' language development. Yet, in many instructional delivery models, mainstream classroom teachers and content-area teachers work separately from ESL teachers (same students, different classrooms and teaching times, sometimes referred to as pull-out instruction). Regardless of which particular title you hold, it is important to communicate regularly with colleagues about the challenges facing your students, and about how to best support them in their learning. Share tools and supports (graphic organizers, word banks, acronyms, and other organizational tools) when possible, so that students have a sense of

continuity from one classroom to the next. If your students thrive when using a particular strategy or tool, make sure their teachers are aware. Likewise, be sure to keep your colleagues informed when you observe students struggle with a particular activity or concept.

3. *Keep a Collection of Differentiated Assessments and Content.* In the examples detailed in this chapter, teachers spend a substantial amount of time differentiating, altering, and creating assessments that are appropriate to use with their EL students. As a teacher, you can reduce your workload if you collaborate and store these assessments so that they are readily available for use in the future, so long as they remain contemporary and appropriate for EL students. Digital storage, such as through a shared drive or with an application such as Google Drive, eliminates excess paper and ensures that these items are not lost. Certainly, this can apply to collecting, sharing, and storing strategy and schema assessments. Regardless of how you go about maintaining such a collection, an atmosphere of collaboration (and organization) is almost certain to reduce unnecessary work.

4. *Advocate for ELs.* There are many circumstances under which ELs will participate in assessments that are not accessible, valid, and/or appropriate for them as individual learners. Because adult stakeholders, and not students themselves, make the overwhelming majority of decisions about education, the students may not able to voice their needs and concerns. The motivation for administering assessments is varied, and the ways in which teachers, parents, and administrators constructively (and respectfully) advocate for ELs differs. Attending school council or committee meetings; volunteering for committees that write, discuss, and review standards; petitioning for appropriate resources and accommodations; welcoming parent involvement in the assessment process; and conducting teacher research to gather data on assessments are just a few ways that you can take action on your students' behalf. Most importantly, you will want to create low-anxiety learning environments where your expectations are reasonable, and learners are able to build confidence in their language abilities. This provides the ELs the support of a teacher who listens and values them, and a classroom where they are comfortable and motivated to learn.

5. *Support ELs on High-Stakes, Standardized Tests.* High-stakes, standardized tests are very different from the assessment activities that you use for summative and formative purposes within your practice. Such tests leave you little opportunity to provide differentiated support to ELs, or to alter the test in any way. You may have no control over how this data is analyzed, used, and shared. Here are some ideas on how you can help prepare students for these:

- Draw attention to the language used on tests (question words, commonly found on Bloom's taxonomy, such as *explain, determine, discuss*), so that

students will have a better understanding of what is being asked of them, and help students to use the language in learning activities (versus using it only during assessments).
- Provide strategy instruction to help students tackle complicated word problems or texts.
- Ensure that students are familiar with any state-approved accommodation tools well in advance of testing (such as bilingual dictionaries or graphic organizers).
- Curb test-related anxiety by stressing the student's success with other tasks (point out that although the state math test is quite difficult, the student has been making significant progress in algebra over the past year).
- Make sure that students know how much their progress (in any area) makes you proud.
- Take the time to really listen to what students think of testing, and to answer their questions about exams, data use, and test-day procedures (students may have misconceptions about testing and/or how their scores affect them personally, putting you in a position to calm unnecessary or unwarranted fears).
- Avoid complaining about tests in ways that are not constructive or helpful, and refrain from projecting your own anxiety about test outcomes onto students.
- Provide emotional "boosters" during testing weeks, such as conducting class outside in nice weather, providing healthy snacks, focusing on pleasure reading/writing, and working with the community to ensure that they are supported outside of school.

Any activity that helps your students to feel more secure about their abilities prior to high-stakes testing activities is worthwhile; anxiety has been shown to have negative effects on testing outcomes (Cassady, 2004; Cassady & Johnson, 2002), confirming what many teachers have observed for years.

RECOMMENDATIONS AND RESOURCES FOR TEACHERS

1. Facilitating exposure to texts written in English and other academic material during authentic reading experiences (in addition to supporting development of students' primary languages) is an effective way to facilitate ELs' developing English literacy. Helping students choose from a large selection of literature allows them to choose reading material that is interesting and accessible to a wide range of English reading abilities. Libraries, whether online, municipal, or within the classroom, are valuable resources.

2. In addition to programming for children and young adults, public libraries may also offer adult ESL classes that would benefit the parents of your ELs, citizenship courses, parenting support groups, and a wide variety of other activities that may be of interest to your students and their families.

3. Offering students help to apply for library cards, particularly if they cannot access an application in the language that they read best, may be a helpful introduction to these resources.

4. School funding organizations, such as DonorsChoose.org, are options that teachers can pursue to increase the text offerings that are appropriate for ELs. First Book (www.firstbook.org), which offers discounted and free books, is another organization that may help schools to acquire appropriate literature and texts, available to staff at Title I schools.

5. Do not overlook thrift stores and organizations such as the Salvation Army. These may offer ways to inexpensively purchase texts needed to make a classroom library more accessible to ELs representing a broad range of English proficiency.

6. In addition to physical book offerings, teachers may want to facilitate student use of technology. Recently, a large selection of ebooks has been made available via the Open eBook app (www.openebooks.net), currently free to students at schools that have Title I funding. StorylineOnline (www.storylineonline.net) features famous readers sharing contemporary and classic picture books via YouTube. The libraries of some public universities and large cities may offer eCards to statewide or regional populations (for example, the Boston Public Library offers eCards to all Massachusetts residents over the age of thirteen), allowing a broader group of people access to online journals and electronic literature.

7. The International Children's Digital Library (www.childrenslibrary.org) offers free online literature in fifty-nine languages. Such resources are wonderful ways to provide students and their families with access to reading material at no cost, provided they have access to the Internet.

8. Teachers, parents, and administrators who wish to stay up to date with information regarding EL assessment and education issues might visit Colorín Colorado (www.colorincolorado.org), a helpful and informative collection of online resources and information.

9. Understanding Language (ell.stanford.edu) provides teaching resources, articles, and other information that may be helpful to teachers and administrators. Share resources from these organizations with your colleagues on current research and teaching tips relevant to teaching ELs.

CHILDREN'S BOOKS CITED

Cleary, B., & Darling, L. (1965). *The mouse and the motorcycle.* New York, NY: William Morrow.
DePaola, T. (1975). *Strega Nona: An old tale.* Englewood Cliffs, NJ: Prentice-Hall.

REFERENCES

Abedi, J., & Gandara, P. (2006). Performance of English language learners as a subgroup in large-scale assessment: Interaction of research and policy. *Educational Measurement: Issues and Practices, 26*(5), 36–46.
Abedi, J., & Levine, H. G. (2013). Fairness in assessment of English learners. *Leadership, 42*(3), 26–28, 38.
Abedi, J., & Linquanti, R. (2012). Issues and opportunities in improving the quality of large scale assessment systems for English language learners. *Understanding Language Conference,* January 13–14, Stanford, CA, Stanford University.
Au, K. H. (1998). Social constructivism and the school literacy learning of students of diverse backgrounds. *Journal of Literacy Research, 30*(2), 297–319.
Beaver, J. (2002). DRA: Developmental reading assessment. Parsippany, NJ: Celebration Press.
Carrell, P. L. (1984). Schema theory and ESL reading: Classroom implications and applications. *The Modern Language Journal, 68*(4), 332–343.
Cassady, J. C. (2004). The influence of cognitive test anxiety across the learning-testing cycle. *Learning and Instruction, 14*(6), 569–592.
Cassady, J. C., & Johnson, R. E. (2002). Cognitive test anxiety and academic performance. *Contemporary Educational Psychology, 27*(2), 270–295.
Compton-Lilly, C. (2006). Identity, childhood culture, and literacy learning: A case study. *Journal of Early Childhood Literacy, 6*(1), 57–76.
Cummins, J. (1979). Cognitive/academic language proficiency, linguistic interdependence, the optimum age question and some other matters. *Working Papers on Bilingualism,* (19), 121–129.
Cummins, J. (1984). *Bilingualism and special educations: Issues in assessment and pedagogy.* Clevedon, UK: Multilingual Matters.
Echevarria, J., Vogt, M., & Short, D. J. (2008). *Making content comprehensible for English Learners: The SIOP model* (3rd ed.). Boston, MA: Allyn & Bacon.
Flippo, R. F. (2014). *Assessing readers: Qualitative diagnosis and instruction* (2nd ed.). New York, NY: Routledge; Newark, DE: International Reading Association.
Flippo, R. F. (with Gaines, R., Rockwell, K. C., Cook, K., & Melia, D.). (2015). *Studying and learning in a high-stakes world: Making tests work for teachers.* Lanham, MD: Rowman & Littlefield.
Flippo, R. F., Holland, D. D., McCarthy, M. T., & Swinning, E. A. (2009). Asking the right questions: How to select an Informal Reading Inventory. *The Reading Teacher, 63*(1), 79–83.
Fountas, I. C. (2008). *Fountas and Pinnell benchmark assessment system 2: Grades 3-8, levels L-Z.* Portsmouth, NH: Heinemann.
Fountas, I. C., & Pinnell, G. S. (2001). *Guiding readers and writers.* Portsmouth, NH: Heinemann.
Fountas, I. C., & Pinnell, G. S. (2007). *Fountas and Pinnell benchmark assessment system 1: Grades K-2, levels A-N.* Portsmouth, NH: Heinemann.
Freeman, D., & Freeman, Y. (2007). *English language learners: The essential guide.* New York, NY: Scholastic.
Gambrell, L. B. (2015). Getting students hooked on the reading habit. *The Reading Teacher, 69*(3), 259–263.

Gándara, P., Maxwell-Jolly, J., & Driscoll, A. (2005). *Listening to teachers of English language learners: A survey of California Teachers' challenges, experiences, and professional development needs*. Santa Cruz, CA: The Center for the Future of Teaching and Learning.

Goodman, Y. M. (1982). Retellings of literature and the comprehension process. *Theory into Practice, 21*(4), 301–307. Retrieved from www.jstor.org/stable/1476356

Hakuta, K. (2014). Assessment of content and language in light of the new standards: Challenges and opportunities for English language learners. *The Journal of Negro Education, 83*(4), 433–441.

Heubert, J. P., & Hauser, R. M. (1999). *High stakes: Testing for tracking, promotion, and graduation. A report of the National Research Council*. Washington, DC: National Academy Press.

Lenski, S. D., Ehlers-Zavala, F., Daniel, M. C., & Sun-Irminger, X. (2006). Assessing English-language learners in mainstream classrooms. *The Reading Teacher, 60*(1), 24–34. Retrieved from www.jstor.org/stable/20204430

Pearson, P. D., Hansen, J., Gordon, C. (1979). The effect of background knowledge on young children's comprehension of explicit and implicit information. *Journal of Literacy Research, 11*(3), 201–209.

Risko, V. J., & Walker-Dalhouse, D. (2007). Tapping students' cultural funds of knowledge to address the achievement gap. *The Reading Teacher, 61*(1), 98–100.

Rothenberg, C., & Fisher, D. (2007). *Teaching English language learners: A differentiated approach*. Upper Saddle River, NJ: Pearson/Merrill Prentice Hall.

U.S. Department of Education, Institute of Education Sciences, National Center for Education Statistics, National Assessment of Educational Progress (NAEP). (2010–2014). Reading Assessments and Mathematics Assessments.

References

Abedi, J., & Gandara, P. (2006). Performance of English language learners as a subgroup in large-scale assessment: Interaction of research and policy. *Educational Measurement: Issues and Practices, 26*(5), 36–46.
Abedi, J., & Levine, H. G. (2013). Fairness in assessment of English learners. *Leadership, 42*(3), 26–28, 38.
Abedi, J., & Linquanti, R. (2012). Issues and opportunities in improving the quality of large scale assessment systems for English language learners. *Understanding Language Conference*, January 13–14, Stanford, CA, Stanford University.
Alvermann, D. E., Unrau, N. J., & Ruddell, R. B. (2013). *Theoretical models and processes of reading* (6th ed.). Newark, DE: International Reading Association.
Amaral, O., Garrison, L., & Klentshy, M. (2002). Helping English language learners increase achievement through inquiry-based science instruction. *Bilingual Research Journal, 26*(2), 213–239.
Assaf, L. C., & Johnson, J. (2014). A call for action: Engaging in purposeful, real-world writing. *Voices from the Middle, 21*(3), 24–33.
Au, K. (2001). Culturally responsive instruction as a dimension of new literacies. *Reading Online, 5*(1), 1–11.
Au, K. H. (1998). Social constructivism and the school literacy learning of students of diverse backgrounds. *Journal of Literacy Research, 30*(2), 297–319.
Bateman, J. A. (2014). *Text and image. A critical introduction to the visual/verbal divide*. New York, NY: Routledge.
Beaver, J. (2002). *DRA: Developmental reading assessment*. Parsippany, NJ: Celebration Press.
Bialystok, E. (2008). Learning as a second language. In A. Rosebery & B. Warren (Eds.), *Teaching science to English language learners* (p. 107). Arlington, VA: NSTA Press.
Bishop, R. S. (1990). Mirrors, windows, and sliding glass doors. *Perspectives: Choosing and Using Books for the Classroom, 6*(3), ix–xi.
Bishop, R. S. (1992). Multicultural literature for children: Making informed choices. In V. Harris (Ed.), *Teaching multicultural literature in grades K-8* (pp. 37–54). Norwood, MA: Christopher-Gordon.
Bosse, S., Jacobs, G., & Anderson, T. L. (2009). Science in the air. *Young Children, 64*, 10–15.
Bourdieu, P. (1987). What makes a social class? On the theoretical and practical existence of groups. *Berkeley Journal of Sociology, 32*, 1–17.
Brassell, D., & Furtado, L. (2008). Enhancing English as a second language students' vocabulary knowledge. *Reading Matrix: An International Online Journal, 8*(1), 111–116.

Brown, H. D. (2007). *Principles of language learning and teaching* (5th ed.). White Plains, NY: Pearson and Longman.
Bruner, J. (1983). *Child's talk: Learning to use language*. Oxford: Oxford University Press.
Canagarajah, S. (2011). Codemeshing in academic writing: Identifying teachable strategies of translanguaging. *The Modern Language Journal, 95*(3), 401–417.
Carrell, P. L. (1984). Schema theory and ESL reading: Classroom implications and applications. *The Modern Language Journal, 68*(4), 332–343.
Cary, S. (2007). *Working with English language learners: Answers to teachers' top ten questions* (2nd ed.). Portsmouth, NH: Heinemann.
Cassady, J. C. (2004). The influence of cognitive test anxiety across the learning-testing cycle. *Learning and Instruction, 14*(6), 569–592.
Cassady, J. C., & Johnson, R. E. (2002). Cognitive test anxiety and academic performance. *Contemporary Educational Psychology, 27*(2), 270–295.
Castro, G. (2015). Helping English language learners succeed in school. *Education Digest, 80*(7), 44–47.
Cazden, C. B. (1997). Curriculum/language contents for bilingual education. In E. J. Briere (Ed.), *Language development in a bilingual setting* (pp. 129–138). Los Angeles, CA: California State University, National Dissemination and Assessment Center (ERIC Document Reproduction Service No. ED224661).
Chen, Y-C., Hand, B., & McDowell, L. (2013). The effects of writing-to-learn activities on elementary students' conceptual understanding: Learning about force and motion through writing to older peers. *Science Education, 97*(5), 745–771.
Ching, S. H. D. (2005). Multicultural children's literature as an instrument of power. *Language Arts, 83*(2), 128–136.
Christie, F., & Derewianka, B. (2008). *School discourse: Learning to write across the years of schooling*. London, UK: Continuum.
Chun, C. (2009). Critical literacies and graphic novels for English-language learners: Teaching Maus. *Journal of Adolescent and Adult Literacy, 53*(2), 144–153. doi:10.1598/JAAL.53.2.5
Colby, S. A., & Lyon, A. F. (2004). Heightening awareness about the importance of using multicultural literature. *Multicultural Education, 11*(3), 24–28.
Compton-Lilly, C. (2006). Identity, childhood culture, and literacy learning: A case study. *Journal of Early Childhood Literacy, 6*(1), 57–76.
Council for Interracial Books for Children. (1974). *10 quick ways to analyze children's books for racism and sexism*. Retrieved from http://alimichael.org/wp-content/uploads/2012/02/10ways-to-analyze-Children-books-for-racism.pdf
Cummins, J. (1979). Cognitive/academic language proficiency, linguistic interdependence, the optimum age question and some other matters. *Working Papers on Bilingualism*, (19), 121–129.
Cummins, J. (1984). *Bilingualism and special educations: Issues in assessment and pedagogy*. Clevedon, UK: Multilingual Matters.
Cummins, J. (1994). The acquisition of English as a second language. In K. Spangenberg-Urbschat & R. Pritchard (Eds.), *Kids come in all languages: Reading instruction for ESL students*. Newark, DE: International Reading Association.
Cummins, J. (2000). *Language, power and pedagogy: Bilingual children in the crossfire*. Clevedon, UK: Multilingual Matters.
Cummins, J. (2000). This place nurtures my spirit: Creating contexts of empowerment in linguistically diverse schools. In R. Phillipson (Ed.), *Rights to language: Equity, power and education* (pp. 249–258). Mahwah, NJ: Lawrence Erlbaum.
Cummins, J. (2003). Reading and the bilingual students: Fact and friction. In G. G. Garcia (Ed.), *English learners: Reaching the highest level of English literacy* (pp. 2–33). Newark, DE: International Reading Association.
Cummins, J. (2008). Technology, literacy, and young second language learners. In L. Lean Parker (Ed.), *Technology-mediated learning environments for young English learners* (pp. 61–98). New York, NY: Lawrence Erlbaum Associates.

Cummins, J. (2009). Pedagogies of choice: Challenging coercive relations of power in classrooms and communities. *International Journal of Bilingual Education and Bilingualism*, 2 (3), 261–271.
Cummins, J. (2011). Literacy engagement. *The Reading Teacher*, 65(2), 142–146.
Cummins, J., & Early, M. (2010). *Identity texts: The collaborative creation of power in multilingual schools*. Staffordshire, UK: Trentham Books Ltd.
Daniel, M. (2016). Critical pedagogy's power in English language teaching. In L. R. Jacobs & C. Hastings (Eds.), *The importance of social justice in English language teaching* (pp. 25–38). Alexandria, VA: TESOL Press.
Daniel, M. (2016). Planning instruction for English language learners: Strategies teachers need to know. In D. Schwarzer & J. Grinberg (Eds.). *Successful teaching: What every novice teacher needs to know* (pp. 89–116). Lanham, MD: Rowman & Littlefield.
DeLeón, L. (2002). Multicultural literature: Reading to develop self-worth. *Multicultural Education*, 10 (2), 49–51.
de Oliveira, L. (2010). Nouns in history: Packaging information, expanding explanations, and structuring reasoning. *The History Teacher*, 43(2), 191–203.
de Oliveira, L., & Iddings, J. (2014). *Genre pedagogy across the curriculum: Theory and application in U.S. classrooms and contexts*. London, UK: Equinox.
de Oliveira, L., & Lan, S. (2014). Writing science in an upper elementary classroom: A genre-based approach to teaching English language learners. *Journal of Second Language Writing*, 25, 23–29.
Dimino, J. A., Taylor, M., & Morris, J. (2015). *Professional learning communities facilitator's guide for the What Works Clearinghouse practice guide: Teaching academic content and literacy to English learners in elementary and middle school* (REL 2015–105). Washington, DC: U.S. Department of Education.
Dixson, A. D., & Fasching-Varner, K. J. (2009). This is how we do it: Helping teachers understand culturally relevant pedagogy in diverse classrooms. In C. Compton-Lilly (Ed.), *Breaking the silence: Recognizing the social and cultural resources students bring to the classroom* (p. 34–48). Newark, DE: International Reading Association.
Dorfman, L. R., & Cappelli, R. (2009). *Nonfiction mentor texts*. Portland, ME: Stenhouse.
Echevarria, J., Vogt, M., & Short, D. J. (2008). *Making content comprehensible for English Learners: The SIOP model* (3rd ed.). Boston, MA: Allyn & Bacon.
Ehlers-Zavala, F. (1999). *Reading an illustrated and non-illustrated story: Dual coding in the foreign language classroom* (Doctoral dissertation, Illinois State University, 1999). Dissertation Abstracts International, 60, 2887.
Ehlers-Zavala, F. (2005). Bilingual reading from a dual coding perspective. In J. Cohen, K. T. McAlister, K. Rolstad, & J. MacSwan (Eds.), *ISB4: Proceedings of the 4th International Symposium on Bilingualism* (pp. 656–662). Somerville, MA: Cascadilla Press.
Ehlers-Zavala, F. (2014). *Dual coding theory (DCT) for the bilingual mind as a theory of L2 reading/writing*. Poster presentation delivered at the 17th World Congress of the International Association of Applied Linguistics (AILA), Brisbane, Australia.
Ehlers-Zavala, F. (2015). *Meeting the reading comprehension challenges of diverse English language learners in K–12. Key contributions from reading research*. Paper presented at the annual meeting of the International Literacy Association (ILA), Saint Louis, MO.
Ehlers-Zavala, F., & Maciejewski, A. (2016). *Mental imagery experienced by both pathway and non-pathway graduate students in an engineering course at a US Research I institution*. Paper presented at the annual meeting of the American Association for Applied Linguistics (AAAL), Orlando, FL.
Erickson, H. L. (2008). *Stirring the head, heart, and soul: Redefining curriculum, instruction, and concept-based teaching*. Thousand Oaks, CA: Corwin Press
Fang, Z. (2010). *Language and literacy in inquiry-based science classrooms, Grades 3-8*. Thousand Oaks, CA: Corwin Press; Arlington, VA: NSTA Press
Fang, Z., & Chapman, Z. (2015). Enhancing English learners' access to disciplinary texts through close reading practices. In M. Daniel & K. Mokhtari (Eds.), *Research-based instruction that makes a difference in English learners' success* (pp. 3–17). Lanham, MD: Rowman and Littlefield.

Fang, Z., & Schleppegrell, M. J. (2008). *Reading in secondary content areas: A language-based pedagogy*. Ann Arbor, MI: University of Michigan Press.

Flippo, R. F. (2014). *Assessing readers: Qualitative diagnosis and instruction* (2nd ed.). New York, NY: Routledge; Newark, DE: International Reading Association.

Flippo, R. F. (with Gaines, R., Rockwell, K. C., Cook, K., & Melia, D.). (2015). *Studying and learning in a high-stakes world: Making tests work for teachers*. Lanham, MD: Rowman & Littlefield.

Flippo, R. F., Holland, D. D., McCarthy, M. T., & Swinning, E. A. (2009). Asking the right questions: How to select an Informal Reading Inventory. *The Reading Teacher, 63*(1), 79–83.

Folse, K. S. (2004). *Vocabulary myths: Applying second language research to classroom teaching*. Ann Arbor, MI: University of Michigan Press.

Fountas, I. C. (2008). *Fountas and Pinnell benchmark assessment system 2: Grades 3-8, levels L-Z*. Portsmouth, NH: Heinemann.

Fountas, I. C., & Pinnell, G. S. (2001). *Guiding readers and writers*. Portsmouth, NH: Heinemann.

Fountas, I. C., & Pinnell, G. S. (2007). *Fountas and Pinnell benchmark assessment system 1: Grades K-2, levels A-N*. Portsmouth, NH: Heinemann.

Freeman, D. E., & Freeman, Y. S. (2001). *Between worlds: Access to second language acquisition* (2nd ed.) Portsmouth, NH: Heinemann.

Freeman, D. E., & Freeman, Y. S. (2007). *English language learners: The essential guide*. New York, NY: Scholastic.

Fry, E. B. (2004). *Dr. Fry's 1000 instant words: The most common words for teaching reading, writing and spelling*. Garden Grove, CA: Teacher Created Resources.

Funk, C., & Rainie, L. (2015). Public and scientists' views on science and society. Pew Research Center. www.pewinternet.org/2015/01/29/public-and-scientists-views-on-science-and-society

Gambrell, L. B. (2015). Getting students hooked on the reading habit. *The Reading Teacher, 69*(3), 259–263.

Gándara, P., Maxwell-Jolly, J., & Driscoll, A. (2005). *Listening to teachers of English language learners: A survey of California Teachers' challenges, experiences, and professional development needs*. Santa Cruz, CA: The Center for the Future of Teaching and Learning.

Gangi, J. M. (2008). The unbearable whiteness of literacy instruction: Realizing the implications of the proficient reader research. *Multicultural Review, 17*(1), 30–35.

Garcia, E., & Lee, O. (2008). Creating culturally responsive learning communities. In A. Rosebery & B. Warren (Eds.), *Teaching science to English language learners* (pp. 147–150). Arlington, VA: NSTA Press.

Garcia, O., & Wei, L. (2014). *Translanguaging: Language, bilingualism, and education*. London, England: Palgrave MacMillan.

Gay, G. (2000). *Culturally responsive teaching: Theory, research, & practice*. New York, NY: Teachers College Press.

Gay, G. (2002). Preparing for culturally responsive teaching. *Journal of Teacher Education, 53*(2), 106–116.

Gee, J. (1992/2014). *The social mind*. Champaign-Urbana, IL: Common Ground.

Gee, J. P. (2008). What is academic literacy? In A. Rosebery & B. Warren (Eds.), *Teaching science to English learners* (pp. 57–70). Arlington, VA: NSTA Press.

Gelman, R., Brenneman, K., Macdonald, G., & Roman., M. (2010). *Preschool pathways to science: Facilitating ways of thinking, talking, doing and understanding*. Baltimore: MD: Brookes Publishing.

Ghiso, M. P., & Campano, G. (2013). Ideologies of language and identity in U.S. children's literature. *Bookbird: A Journal of International Children's Literature, 51*(3), pp. 47–55.

Gibbons, P. (2015). *Scaffolding language scaffolding learning: Teaching second language learners in the mainstream classroom*. Portsmouth, NH: Heinemann.

González, N. (2005). Beyond culture: The hybridity of funds of knowledge. In N. González, L. Moll, & C. Amanti (Eds.), *Funds of knowledge: Theorizing practices in households, communities, and classrooms* (pp. 29–46). Mahwah, NJ: Lawrence Erlbaum.

González, N., Moll, L., & Amanti, C. (Eds.) (2005). *Funds of knowledge for teaching in Latino households*. Mahwah, NJ: Lawrence Erlbaum

Goodman, Y. M. (1982). Retellings of literature and the comprehension process. *Theory into Practice, 21*(4), 301–307. Retrieved from www.jstor.org/stable/1476356

Grabe, W. (2009). *Reading in a second language. Moving from theory to practice*. New York, NY: Cambridge University Press.

Graham, S., & Perin, D. (2007). *Writing next: Effective strategies to improve writing of adolescents in middle and high schools*. Washington, DC: Alliance for Excellent Education.

Graves, D. H. (2002). *Testing is not teaching*. Portsmouth, NH: Heinemann.

Gray, E. S. (2009). The importance of visibility: Students' and teachers' criteria for selecting African American literature. *The Reading Teacher, 62*(6), 472–481.

Guthrie, J. T., McGough, K., Bennett, L., & Rice, M. E. (1996). Concept-oriented reading instruction to develop motivational and cognitive aspects of reading. In L. Baker, P. Afflerbach, & D. Reinking (Ed.), *Developing engaged readers in school and home communities* (pp. 165–190). Mahwah, NJ: Erlbaum

Guthrie, J. T., & Wigfield, A. (2000). Engagement and motivation in reading. In M. L. Kamil, P. B. Mosenthal, P. D. Pearson, & R. Barr (Eds.), *Handbook of reading research* (Vol. 3, pp. 403–422). Mahwah, NJ: Lawrence Erlbaum Associates.

Guthrie, J. T., Wigfield, A., Barbosa, P., Perencevich, K. C., Taboada, A., Davis, M. H., . . . Tonks, S. (2004). Increasing reading comprehension and engagement through concept-oriented reading instruction. *Journal of Educational Psychology, 96*(3), 403–423.

Gutiérrez-Clellen, V., Simon-Cereijido, G., & Sweet, M. (2012). Predictors of second language acquisition in Latino children with specific language impairment. *American Journal of Speech-Language Pathology, 21*(1), 64–77.

Hadaway, N. L., & Young, T. A., (2006). Negotiating meaning through writing. In T. A. Young & N. L. Hadaway (Eds.), *Supporting the literacy development of English learners: Increasing success in all classrooms* (pp. 150–167). Newark, DE: International Reading Association.

Hakuta, K. (2014). Assessment of content and language in light of the new standards: Challenges and opportunities for English language learners. *The Journal of Negro Education, 83*(4), 433–441.

Hakuta, K., Butler, Y. G., & Witt, D. (2000). *How long does it take English learners to attain proficiency?* Santa Barbara, CA: University of California Linguistic Minority Research Institute.

Hammond, J. (2008). Intellectual challenge and ESL students: Implications of quality teaching initiatives. *Australian Journal of Language and Literacy, 31*(2), 128.

Haneda, M. (2009). Learning about the past and preparing for the future: A longitudinal investigation of a grade 7 'sheltered' social studies class. *Language and Education, 23*(4), 335–352.

Heflin, B. R., & Barksdale-Ladd, M. A. (2001). African American children's literature that helps students find themselves: Selection guidelines for grades K-3. *The Reading Teacher, 54*(8), 810–819.

Herrera, S. G., & Murry, K. G. (2016). *Mastering ESL/EFL methods* (3rd ed.). New York, NY: Pearson.

Heubert, J. P., & Hauser, R. M. (1999). *High stakes: Testing for tracking, promotion, and graduation. A report of the National Research Council*. Washington, DC: National Academy Press.

Horizon Research. (2012). 2012 national survey of science and mathematics educational highlights report. Retrieved on March 20, 2016, from www.horizon-research.com/2012-national-survey-of-science-and-mathematics-education-highlights-report-2

Howard, T. C. (2003). Culturally relevant pedagogy: Ingredients for critical teacher reflection. *Theory into Practice, 42*(3), 195–202.

Hudelson, S. Y., & Serna, I. (1994). Beginning literacy in English in a whole-language bilingual program. In A. Flurkey & R. Meyer (Eds.), *Under the whole language umbrella: Many cultures, many voices* (pp. 278–294). Urbana, IL: National Teachers of English.

Hughes-Hassell, S., Barkley, H., & Koehler, E. (2009). Promoting equity in children's literacy instruction: Using a critical race theory framework to examine transitional books. *School Library Media Research, 12*, 1–20.

Hyland, K. (2004). *Genre and second language writing*. Ann Arbor, MI: University of Michigan.

Hyland, K. (2007). Genre pedagogy: language, literacy and L2 writing instruction. *Journal of Second Language Writing, 16*, 148–164.

Illinois State Board of Education (ISBE). (2014). *Illinois learning standards: Social science*. Retrieved from www.isbe.net/ils/social_science/standards.htm.

Ivarsson, J., Linderoth, J., & Säljö, R. (2009). Representations in practices: A socio-cultural approach to multimodality in reasoning. In C. Jewitt (Ed.), *The Routledge handbook of multimodal analysis* (pp. 201–212). New York, NY: Routledge.

Kayi-Aydar, H. (2013). Scaffolding language learning in an academic ESL classroom. *ELT Journal, 67*(3), 324–335.

Kelley, M., Wilson, N. S., & Koss, M. D. (2012). Using young adult literature to motivate and engage the disengaged. In J. A. Hayn & J. S. Kaplan (Eds.), *Teaching young adult literature today: Insights, considerations and perspectives for the classroom teacher* (pp. 77–98). Lanham, MD: Rowman & Littlefield

Key, C., Hand, B., Prain, V., & Collins, S. (1999). Using the science writing heuristic as a tool for learning from laboratory investigations in secondary science. *Journal of Research in Science Teaching, 36*(10), 1065–1084.

Kohnen, A. (2013). The authenticity spectrum: The case of a science journalism writing project. *English Journal, 102*(5), 28–34.

Krashen, S. (2004). *The power of reading*. Portsmouth, NH: Heinemann.

Krashen, S. (2013). *Second language acquisition: Theory, applications, and some conjectures*. Cambridge, UK: Cambridge University Press.

Kuhn, D. (2010). Teaching and learning science as argument. *Science Education, 94*, 810–824.

Landt, S. M. (2011). Integration of multicultural literature in primary grade language arts curriculum. *Journal of Multiculturalism in Education, 7*, 1–27.

Langer de Ramirez, L. (2010). *Empower English language learners with tools from the web*. Thousand Oaks, CA: Corwin Press.

Larson, J., & Marsh, J. (2005). *Making literacy real: Theories and practices for learning and teaching*. Thousand Oaks, CA: Sage.

Jacobs, H. H., Randolph, B., & LeVasseur, M. (2003). *Latin America*. Glenview, IL: Prentice Hall.

Lawrence, J. (1993). *The great migration: An American story*. New York, NY: The Museum of Modern Art.

Lee, O., & Buxton, C. A. (2013). Integrating science and English proficiency for English language learners. *Theory into Practice, 52*(1), 36–42.

Lee, O., Quinn, H., & Valdes, G. (2013). Science and language for English language learners in relation to Next Generation Science Standards and with implications for Common Core State Standards for English Language Arts and Mathematics. *Educational Researcher, 20*(10), 1–11.

Lee, S. (2008). *Wave*. San Francisco, CA: Chronicle Books.

Lenski, S. D., Ehlers-Zavala, F., Daniel, M. C., & Sun-Irminger, X. (2006). Assessing English-language learners in mainstream classrooms. *The Reading Teacher, 60*(1), 24–34. Retrieved from www.jstor.org/stable/20204430

Levine, L. N., & McCloskey, M. L. (2013). *Teaching English language and content in mainstream classes: One class, many paths* (2nd ed.). New York, NY: Pearson.

Lewis, J., & Aydin, A. (2013). *The march: Book one*. Marietta, GA: Top Shelf Productions.

Lewis, J., & Aydin, A. (2015). *The march: Book two*. Marietta, GA: Top Shelf Productions.

Lewis, J., & Aydin, A. (2016). *The march: Book three*. Marietta, GA: Top Shelf Productions.

Lohfink, G. (2010). The nature of Mexican American third graders' engagement with culturally relevant picture books. *Bilingual Research Journal, 33*(3), 346–363.

Lucas, T., Villegas, A. M., & Freedson-Gonzalez, M. (2008). Linguistically responsive teacher education preparing classroom teachers to teach English language learners. *Journal of Teacher Education, 59*(4), 361–373.
Martinez, M., Koss, M. D., Johnson, N. J. (2016). Meeting characters in Caldecotts: What does this mean for today's readers? *The Reading Teacher, 70*(1), 19–28.
Martinez-Roldán, C. (2005). The inquiry acts of bilingual children in literature discussions. *Language Arts, 83*(1), 22–32.
McNair, J. C. (2010). Classic African American children's literature. *The Reading Teacher, 64*(2), 96–105.
Mercer, N., Dawes, L., & Staarman, J. K. (2009). Dialogic teaching in the primary science classroom. *Language and Education, 23*(4), 353–369.
Miller, G. A., & Gildea, P. M. (1987). How children learn words. *Scientific American, 257*(3), 94–97.
Misco, T., & Castañeda, M. (2009). "Now, what should I do for English language learners?" Reconceptualizing social studies curriculum design for ELLs. *Educational Horizons, 87*(3), 183–189.
Moje, E. (2008). Foregrounding the disciplines in secondary literacy teaching and learning: A call for change. *Journal of Adolescent and Adult Literacy, 52*(2), 96–107.
Montgomery, W. (2001). Creating culturally responsive, inclusive classrooms. *Teaching Exceptional Children, 33*(4), 4–9.
Morrison, K. A., Robbins, H. H., & Rose, D. G. (2008). Operationalizing culturally relevant pedagogy: A synthesis of classroom based research. *Equity & Excellence in Education, 41*(4), 433–452.
Nation, I. S. P. (2009). *Teaching ESL/EFL reading and writing.* New York, NY: Routledge.
Nation, P., & Waring, R. (2004). *Second language reading and incidental vocabulary learning.* Retrieved on March 31, 2016, from www.robwaring.org/papers/various/waring_120304.pdf
National Research Council. (1996). *National Science Education Standards.* Washington, DC: National Academy Press.
National Research Council. (2012). *A framework for K-12 science education: Practices, crosscutting concepts, and core ideas.* Washington, DC: The National Academies Press.
Nodelman, P. (1988). *Words about pictures.* Athens, GA: The University of Georgia Press.
Noonan, E. (2013). The history textbook, born digital. *Radical History Review, 117,* 131–138. doi: 10.1215/01636545-2210658
Osborne, J. (2010). Arguing to learn in science: The role of collaborative, critical discourse. *Science,* 328, 463–466.
Painter, C., Martin, J. R., & Unsworth, L. (2013). *Reading visual narratives.* Bristol, CT: Equinox.
Paivio, A. (1971). *Imagery and verbal processes.* New York, NY: Holt, Reinhart, & Winston.
Paivio, A. (1990). *Mental representations. A dual coding approach.* New York, NY: Oxford University Press.
Paivio, A., & Desrochers, A. (1980). A dual coding approach to bilingual memory. *Canadian Journal of Psychology, 34,* 388–399.
Paquette, K. R., & Rieg, S. A. (2008). Using music to support the literacy development of young English language learners. *Early Childhood Education Journal, 36*(3), 227–232.
Pearson, P. D., Hansen, J., Gordon, C. (1979). The effect of background knowledge on young children's comprehension of explicit and implicit information. *Journal of Literacy Research, 11*(3), 201–209.
Peregoy, S. F., & Boyle, O. F. (2013). *Reading, writing, and learning in ESL: A resource book for teaching K-12 English learners* (6th ed.). Boston, MA: Pearson.
Potter, B. (1972). *The tale of Peter Rabbit.* New York, NY: Dover.
Pytash, K. E., & Ferdig, R. E. (2014). *Exploring technology for writing and writing instruction.* Hershey, PA: IGI Global.
Qi, Y. (2015). *Learning to write in science: A study of English language learners' writing experience in sixth-grade science classrooms.* Unpublished doctoral dissertation, University of Florida, Gainesville, Florida.

Quinn, H., Lee, O., & Valdés, G. (2012) Language demands and opportunities in relation research. *Human Resource Magazine Review, 20*, 115–131. Retrieved on March 14, 2016, from www.elsevier.com/locate/humres

Read, S. (2010). A model for scaffolding writing instruction: IMSCI. *The Reading Teacher, 64*(1), 47–52.

Richards, G. (2009). Book review: Technology-mediated learning environments for young English learners. *Educational Technology & Society, 12*(2), 334–336.

Risko, V. J., & Walker-Dalhouse, D. (2007). Tapping students' cultural funds of knowledge to address the achievement gap. *The Reading Teacher, 61*(1), 98–100.

Rivard, L. P., & Straw, S. B. (2000). The effect of talk and writing on learning science: An exploratory study. *Science Education, 84*, 566–593.

Rodrigo, V., Krashen, S., & Gribbons, B. (2004). The effectiveness of two comprehensible-input approaches to foreign language instruction at the intermediate level. *System, 32*(1), 53.

Rose, D., & Martin, J. (2012). *Learning to write/reading to learn: Genre, knowledge and pedagogy in the Sydney School*. Bristol, CT: Equinox.

Rosenblatt, L. M. (1978). *The reader, the text, the poem: The transactional theory of the literary work*. Carbondale, IL: Southern Illinois University Press.

Rothenberg, C., & Fisher, D. (2007). *Teaching English language learners: A differentiated approach*. Upper Saddle River, NJ: Pearson/Merrill Prentice Hall.

Rowsell, J., Kress, J., Pahl, K., & Street, B. (2013). The social practice of multimodal reading: A new literacy studies—multimodal perspective on reading. In R. B. Ruddell and N. J. Unrau (Eds.), *Theoretical models and processes of reading* (5th ed., pp. 1182–1207). Newark, DE: International Reading Association.

Rugg, H. (1936). *American life and the school curriculum: Next steps towards schools of living*. Boston, MA: Ginn and Co.

Ryan, A. M., & Patrick, H. (2001). The classroom social environment and changes in adolescents' motivation and engagement during middle school. *American Educational Research Journal, 38*(2), 437–460.

Sadoski, M., & Paivio, A. (2001). *Imagery and text: A dual coding theory of reading and writing*. Mahwah, NJ: Lawrence Erlbaum Associates.

Sadoski, M., & Paivio, A. (2004). A dual coding theoretical model of reading. In R. B. Ruddell and N. J. Unrau (Eds.), *Theoretical models and processes of reading* (5th ed., pp. 1329–1362). Newark, DE: International Reading Association.

Sadoski, M., & Paivio, A. (2013). *Imagery and text: A dual coding theory of reading and writing* (2nd ed.). New York, NY: Routledge.

Sadoski, M., Paivio, A., & Goetz, E. T. (1991). A critique to schema theory in reading and a dual coding alternative. *Reading Research Quarterly, 26*(4), 251–271.

Samway, K. D. (2006). *When English language learners write: Connecting research to practice, K-8*. Portsmouth, NH: Heinemann.

Schleppegrell, M. (1998). Grammar as resource: Writing a description. *Research in the Teaching of English, 32*(2), 182–209.

Schleppegrell, M. (2004). *The language of schooling: A functional linguistics perspective*. Mahwah, NJ: Lawrence Erlbaum Associates.

Seah, L., Clarke, D., & Hart, C. (2011). Understanding students' language use about expansion through analyzing their lexicogrammatical resources. *Science Education, 95*(5), 852–876.

Sendak, M. (2012). *Where the wild things are*. New York, NY: HarperCollins.

Sipress, J., & Voelker, D. (2011). The end of the history survey course: The rise and fall of the coverage model. *The Journal of American History, 97*(4), 1050–1066.

Snow, C. (2008). What is the vocabulary of science? In A. Rosebery & B. Warren (Eds.), *Teaching science to English language learners* (pp. 71-84). Arlington, VA: NSTA Press.

Souto-Manning, M. (2009). Negotiating culturally responsive pedagogy through multicultural children's literature: Towards critical democratic literacy practices in a first grade classroom. *Journal of Early Childhood Literacy, 9*(1), 50–74.

Spiegelman, A. (2011). *Maus: A survivor's tale*. New York, NY: Pantheon Books.

Stead, T., & Hoyt, L. (2012). *A guide to teaching nonfiction writing*. Portsmouth, NH: Heinemann.

Szpara, M., & Ahmad, I. (2007). Supporting English-language learners in social studies class: Results from a study of high school teachers. *The Social Studies, 98*(5), 189–196.
Takaki, R. (2008). *A different mirror: A history of multicultural America*. New York, NY: Back Bay Books, Little, Brown.
Taylor, B. M., Pearson, P. D., Peterson, D. S., & Rodriguez, M. C. (2003). Reading growth in high-poverty classrooms: The influence of teacher practices that encourage cognitive engagement in literacy learning. *The Elementary School Journal, 104*(1), 3–28.
TESOL/NCATE Teacher Standards Committee. (2009). *Standards for the recognition of initial TESOL programs in P-12 ESL teacher education (2010)*. Alexandria, VA: Teachers of English for Speakers of Other Languages. Retrieved from www.tesol.org
Thomas, W. P., & Collier, V. P. (1999). Accelerated schooling for English language learners. *Educational Leadership, 56*(7), 46–49.
Trelease, J. (2006). *The read aloud handbook*. (6th ed.). New York, NY: Penguin Books.
U.S. Census Bureau. (2013). Retrieved from www.census.gov/2013census/data
U.S. Department of Education, Institute of Education Sciences, National Center for Education Statistics, National Assessment of Educational Progress (NAEP). (2010–2014). Reading Assessments and Mathematics Assessments.
Underwood, J. D. M., & Farrington-Flint, L. (2015). *Learning and the E-Generation*. Malden, MA: Wiley-Blackwell.
Underwood, J. D. M., & Underwood, G. (1990). *Computers and learning: Helping children acquire thinking skills*. Oxford, UK: Blackwell.
Van Staden, A. (2011). Put reading first: Positive effects of direct instruction and scaffolding for ESL learners struggling with reading. *Perspectives in Education, 29*(4), 10–21.
Virginia Board of Education. (2008). *History and social science standards of learning for Virginia public schools*. Richmond, VA: Virginia Department of Education.
Vygotsky, L. S. (1978). *Mind in society: The development of higher psychological processes*. Cambridge, MA: Harvard University Press.
Vygotsky, L. S. (1986). *Thought and language*. Cambridge, MA: MIT Press.
Wang, S., & Noe, R. (2010). Knowledge sharing: A review and direction for future research. *Human resource management review, 20*, 115–131.
Warren, B., & Rosebery, A. (2008). Using everyday experience to teach science. In A. Rosebery & B. Warren (Eds.), *Teaching science to English language learners* (pp. 39–50). Arlington, VA: NSTA Press.
Watts-Taffe, S., & Truscott, D. M. (2000). Focus on research using what we know about language and literacy development for ESL students in the mainstream classroom. *Language Arts, 77*(3), 258–265.
WIDA Can Do Descriptors. Retrieved from www.wida.us/standards/CAN_DO
Williams, C., & Pilonieta, P. (2012). Using interactive writing instruction with kindergarten and first-grade English language learners. *Early Childhood Education Journal, 40*(3), 145–150.
Williams, E. (1970). *From Columbus to Castro: A history of the Caribbean, 1492-1969*. New York, NY: Vintage Books.
Wolf, S. (2004). *Interpreting literature with children*. Mahwah, NJ: Lawrence Erlbaum.
Wolters, C., & Pintrich, P. (1998). Contextual differences in student motivation and self-regulated learning in mathematics, English, and social studies classrooms. *Instructional Science, 26*(1–2), 27–47.
Yoon, B., Simpson, A., & Haag, C. (2010). Assimilation ideology: Critically examining underlying messages in multicultural literature. *Journal of Adolescent & Adult Literacy, 54*(2), 109–118.
Yore, L. (2004). Why do future scientists need to study the language arts? In W. Saul (Ed.), *Crossing borders in literacy and science: Perspectives on theory and practice* (71–107). Newark, DE: International Reading Association.
Yore, L., Hand, B., Florence, M. (2004). Scientists views of science, models of writing, and science writing practices. *Journal of Research in Science Teaching, 41*(4), 338–369.
Young, C., & Rasinski, T. V. (2013). Student-produced movies as a medium for literacy development. *Reading Teacher, 66*(8), 670–675.

Zeigler, L. L., & John, J. L. (2005). *Visualization: Using mental images to strengthen comprehension*. Dubuque, IA: Kendall Hunt.

About the Editor

Dr. Mayra C. Daniel, professor in the Department of Curriculum and Instruction at Northern Illinois University, is the coordinator for the Bilingual/English as a Second Language Program for NIU's College of Education. She recently finished serving as an elected member of the TESOL Organization's Nominating Committee. She has been chair of several committees of the International Literacy Association, such as the Literacy, Diversity, and Multiculturalism Committee.

Daniel's research and teaching center on preparing and empowering educators who work with plurilingual and pluricultural learners in the United States, Guatemala, and Ecuador. She is committed to helping teachers plan culturally responsive instruction and become advocates for English learners and their communities. In her work she has focused on formative assessment, bilingual education, technology in literacy, and instructional methodologies for classrooms with English learners.

She has presented her research at numerous national and international conferences. Three of her more recent publications are book chapters that address the topics of social justice, cultural capital in English language teaching, and preparing novice teachers to work with English learners: "Critical Pedagogy's Power in English Language Teaching" and "Exploring Perceptions of Gender Roles in English Language Teaching" (in L. R. Jacobs & C. Hastings, *The Importance of Social Justice in English Language Teaching*, TESOL Press, 2016), and "Planning Instruction for English Language Learners: Strategies Teachers Need to Know" (in D. Schwarzer & J. Grinberg, *Successful Teaching: What Every Novice Teacher Needs to Know*, Rowman & Littlefield, 2016). In 2015 she co-edited *Research Based Instruction That Makes a Difference in English Learners' Success* (Rowman & Littlefield).

List of Contributors

Brittany Adams, University of Florida
Suzanne Chapman, University of Florida
Fabiola Ehlers Zavala, Colorado State University
Zhihui Fang, University of Florida
Maureen Fennessy, University of Florida
Caitlin Gallingane, University of Florida
Carolyn Riley, Northern Illinois University
Rodney Fitzgerald, Northern Illinois University
Rona F. Flippo, University of Massachusetts
Soowon Jo, University of Florida
Kathrine Crane Rockwell, Medford Public Schools
Melanie Koss, Northern Illinois University
Teresa Kruger, Rockford Public Schools
Cuiying Li, Chongqing Jiaotong University, China

www.ingramcontent.com/pod-product-compliance
Lightning Source LLC
Chambersburg PA
CBHW030115010526
44116CB00005B/259